unatoned

unatoned

Brent LaPorte

a memoir

Published by ECW Press
665 Gerrard Street East
Toronto, Ontario, Canada M4M 1Y2
416-694-3348 / info@ecwpress.com

Editor for the Press: Michael Holmes
Cover design: Trevor Campbell
Cover photos from the author's personal collection

To the best of his abilities, the author has related
experiences, places, people, and organizations
from his memories of them. In order to protect
the privacy of others, he has, in some instances,
changed the names of certain people and details of
events and places.

LIBRARY AND ARCHIVES CANADA CATALOGUING IN
PUBLICATION

Title: Unatoned : a memoir / Brent LaPorte.

Names: LaPorte, Brent, author.

Identifiers: Canadiana (print) 20200402757 |
Canadiana (ebook) 20200402854

ISBN 978-1-77041-504-1 (softcover)
ISBN 978-1-77305-657-9 (EPUB)
ISBN 978-1-77305-658-6 (PDF)
ISBN 978-1-77305-659-3 (Kindle)

Subjects: LCSH: LaPorte, Brent. | LCSH:
LaPorte, Brent—Family. | LCSH: Fathers and
sons—Canada—Biography. | LCSH: Adult
children of alcoholics—Canada—Biography. |
CSH: Authors, Canadian (English)—Biography. |
LCGFT: Autobiographies.

Classification: LCC PS8623.A7368 Z46 2021 |
DDC C818/.603—dc23

The publication of *Unatoned* has been generously supported by the Canada Council for the Arts and is
funded in part by the Government of Canada. *Nous remercions le Conseil des arts du Canada de son soutien.
Ce livre est financé en partie par le gouvernement du Canada.* We acknowledge the support of the Ontario Arts
Council (OAC), an agency of the Government of Ontario, which last year funded 1,965 individual artists and
1,152 organizations in 197 communities across Ontario for a total of $51.9 million. We also acknowledge the
contribution of the Government of Ontario through the Ontario Book Publishing Tax Credit, and through
Ontario Creates for the marketing of this book.

ONTARIO ARTS COUNCIL
CONSEIL DES ARTS DE L'ONTARIO
an Ontario government agency
un organisme du gouvernement de l'Ontario

Canada Council   Conseil des arts
for the Arts   du Canada

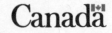

PRINTED AND BOUND IN CANADA   PRINTING: MARQUIS   5   4   3   2   1

MIX
Paper from
responsible sources
FSC® C103567

To my mother, Heather:
Thank you for showing me the value of hard work,
keeping a positive attitude and, most importantly,
that growing up, while we may not have had much,
we always had each other.

TABLE OF CONTENTS

My father's house shines hard and bright
It stands like a beacon calling me in the night
Calling and calling so cold and alone
Shining 'cross this dark highway where our sins lie
    unatoned

                                    — Bruce Springsteen

PREFACE

Writing this book was more difficult than I ever imagined. I'd stored these painful memories away for so long that they did not exist in my present mind. Most difficult was having to return, to these places and times, to allow myself to share these experiences honestly, in ways that were as raw as when they were happening. As a result, much of the emotion expressed in this book comes from a confused, tortured, damaged and angry child.

My views and opinions may be confusing, and misunderstood by some readers, and that's okay—it really is. To write a book about suicide and its reverberations, I had to share the feelings of those left behind that, up until now, may not have been expressed.

Please allow the adult me to ask for your indulgence in the nine-year-old me.

IT BEGINS

I was maybe five years old and living with my mom, brother and three sisters in a basement apartment in Sudbury, Ontario.

The winters were brutal. Cold beyond belief. The snowfall was unrelenting.

It was the mid '70s.

We were on welfare, had little money and fewer options.

We'd settled in the Flour Mill District amid other families who could not afford to be anywhere else. Our basement apartment was the Canadian version of a cold water flat in the Bronx.

The apartment had three rooms. A kitchen and two bedrooms. Our mother slept in one bedroom and the five of us slept in the other. The windows to our rooms faced the road. If you stood on one of the beds, you could look out and see King Street.

I was in bed and was awakened by a pounding at our door. It was not a long run for me to see what was going on. I saw and heard my mother from across the small kitchen tell this man she would not let him in. I could also hear the madman on the other side of the door, demanding entry. The man on the other side of the door was my father.

My mother was terrified.

We all were.

We knew what he was capable of—we had seen it.

Five young children and one young mother trapped in a basement apartment, with no telephone and no means of escape. We were under attack.

He was loud. Probably drunk. Yet somehow he convinced my mother to open the door a crack so he could talk to her.

She did.

The chain lock was on so he could not get in.

Or so we thought.

Once my mother had opened the door a sliver, he shoved his right arm through, reaching, trying to get a hold of her. She jumped back, yet he continued to grab at thin air. His arm just flailing around through this tiny opening, grasping for anything he could get his powerful hand on, all the while yelling what he was going to do to my mother when he got through.

The flimsy chain was no match for his drunken brute strength as evidenced by splinters of wood on the floor and the feeble lock hanging on what was left of the broken door frame. The image of him grabbing my mother by her hair and spinning her around that small apartment will never leave me. I do not remember what he said, but I know what he did. He beat this woman brutally in front of his five children. This was not the first time, but for me, it remains the most violent and vivid. He had not come home from work, as he had done in the past, angry about supper; no, he'd broken into what was supposed to be our home and tore down our last line of defence, right before our eyes.

She did nothing to deserve this. Other than being born, we did nothing to deserve this.

All my mother had done was remove her children from an abusive situation, and the result was the beating of a lifetime.

During my time as a police officer, I saw many disturbing things. Nothing I witnessed or experienced affected me the way this did.

Thankfully, another single mother in the building had the means to pay for a telephone, and she called the police. It took six cops to take my dad off of my mother and out of that cramped apartment to the street where their cars were parked. I know this because I watched them take my dad out in handcuffs. I stood on my bed and pleaded along with my brother and sisters through the window for the officers to leave my father alone as they did their job and dragged him to a waiting police car.

It was awful. Watching my mother get beaten by my father and watching my father struggle with the police.

I've never been the same.

I'll never be the same.

Innocence lost? I'm not sure I ever had it. Life wasn't good before that night, and it didn't get any better for a long, long time.

The premise for this book came to me one night while I was walking up the stairs to the loft above my garage to do some writing. Ascending, I had the strange feeling that my father was going to be sitting at my desk waiting for me. That image raised the hairs on my arms and the back of my neck. I knew it wasn't possible, but still, I hesitated.

The rational part of my brain urged me on and told me that because he killed himself when I was nine he couldn't possibly be sitting at my desk smoking a cigarette waiting to talk to me. The irrational part of my brain compelled me to keep climbing those stairs because if he *was* sitting there smoking a cigarette, then he had a lot of questions to answer . . .

I never saw him dead, you know. Never.

I was not allowed to go to his wake and, honestly, cannot even remember if there was a funeral. I only remember aunts and uncles from my mom's side in our small kitchen, eyes red and puffy, crying and saying, "It didn't even look like him."

A bullet to the head will do that. I will add that in speaking with one of my aunts years later about this very scene, she had been just as relieved as my mom that he was dead. Quite a tribute. Apparently he was not just a monster to his immediate family.

Mom thought I was too young to go to his wake. Maybe she thought it might be too much for a nine-year-old to handle. Maybe she was right; but for years I did not believe he was dead. I thought the entire thing was an elaborate hoax being played to keep me away from him. It would have been quite the hoax. I don't know for sure, but I guess this is evidence of the narcissism of a nine-year-old, thinking the entire world revolves around him.

Oddly, I had a special bond with him—sure he was a monster, but he was my monster.

So, when I mentioned this eerie feeling from that night to Michael, my editor and, more importantly, my friend, he said, "That's your next book."

I replied, "No one wants to read a book about a conversation between Brent LaPorte and his dead father." I'm not a famous athlete, musician or author. Sure I published a novel in 2010, but I'm hardly a household name. No one is looking to read about me or my life.

His reply was simply, "Brent, I'd like to have that conversation with my father—and he's still alive."

I began to write. It was mostly fiction, with a lot of real events mixed in.

People began asking when my next book was coming out, and I had to answer that it was in fact written but I didn't know when . . . And then it went on for four years.

Now, I should have prefaced this with the fact that I knew when I submitted it that it was not ready for publication. A lot of editing was required, and frankly, I've been pretty consumed with rebuilding my financial life after a couple of bad business decisions and hadn't had the heart to completely rewrite the first section.

But there is more.

Michael's father had been fighting one of the most courageous battles with cancer I've ever known. His father had been ill pretty much as long as I've known Michael.

Prior to his father's death, I'd asked Michael a few times about the status of the book, and his answers were always a little vague. Protecting me, I believe, from the harsh criticism that an editor has to provide his author.

But there is still a little more.

Michael and I had become close. We know more about each other's struggles, successes and plain old daily life than either of us care to admit.

We put our friendship ahead of our professional relationship. I wouldn't have it any other way. You can always find another editor. You cannot always find another friend— truly devoted—like Michael.

So, that's all nice—but what of it?

I still had to address this editorial issue with him, and finally, one night, each of us with a belly full of beer, lungs full of cigar smoke, I asked him why the book was taking so long.

His honest answer was that he was too close to it.

I was too close to him, and he felt my pain.

Further, he was too close to the story about a long-overdue conversation between father and son.

His father was dying.

Mine was dead.

Easy for me to write about; hard for him to read, to think about as he was making the hour-and-a-half drive multiple times a week to see his sick father and still healthy mother. He is that kind of man. That kind of son.

Unfortunately, I had happened to write a book that directly affected my editor and friend.

"Of all the gin joints in the world . . ." This was a collision of cosmic proportions. At least personally.

Crazy, but true.

Michael, you will be the first to read this, and you can ask me to take this out and I will, but I think this is as important to the information that I share as anything else I write.

I share this relationship with the world to let everyone know that strangely enough, we are all human. We all experience pain, joy, sadness and grief. Cops, nurses, teachers and, yes, even editors.

We all bleed.

It is far easier to treat the wounds on the outside than on the inside.

It is for this reason that I decided to rewrite this book.

I hope it works. More importantly, I hope it helps.

This all began with a story that would lead me toward a meeting and a conversation between me and my dead father—that my father had returned from the grave to send me a message and prevent me from following his path. What kind of a premise is that for a novel? Not a very good one, based on my first attempt. We would hopefully have had an imaginary natural conversation about our past, me asking him why he did what he did, and then me answering for him why he did what he did. Mostly fiction, with real events mixed in.

You know, everyone I spoke with about the premise of the story told me that this was probably some sort of therapy for me. I disagreed with them. Seriously, I felt that I had completely reconciled with the fact that when I was nine years old my father blew his brains all over the walls and ceiling of his mobile home. He had problems, and the answers were found in a bottle of rum and a box of .222 shells. Well, one shell, really.

In retrospect—one poorly written unpublished novel later—these people may have had a point.

Am I really looking for his side of the story? Maybe. Of course, I may just be looking to have my say. To tell him and everyone else my thoughts and ask the questions that have been plaguing me my entire life.

WHY DID YOU DO IT?

Why did you do it, Dad? Did you not know the devastation that one bullet could leave behind? You didn't just shoot yourself. You shot me. You shot Mom. You shot my brother. You shot my sisters. You shot our entire family. You shot your friends. You shot all of us, you selfish son of a bitch.

In one moment, you changed all of our lives. Did you ever think of that? I'm guessing not. You never thought of us in your life, so why would you think of us when you were about to die.

I am aware that mental health professionals will take issue with my questions about why you did it. To them I say, I *know* my father was mentally ill. I *know* he was an alcoholic. I *know* that in 1979 there was very little help available to someone with his issues. Knowing all of this does not ease the pain and suffering that my family and I have gone through. It's very hard at nine years old to be understanding of the man who just shattered your entire life. I don't say that lightly. I was devastated. Maybe I still am.

When the attempt at a novel failed, I took a hard left on this project. I decided to be more real. More honest. As honest as one can be and still maintain some sense of self-respect. I am not going to hide my true feelings behind some literary smokescreen. Hopefully this honesty will bring some closure for me, a better experience to anyone reading an account of my life of living with an abusive alcoholic, and some comfort to anyone who has lived through or is living in a similar situation.

While I am writing this for me, I am also writing this for you. You would not have picked up this book if you did not feel that this small tome may offer you something. Anything. A tiny peek into the mind of someone like you. I'm writing this because I'm not sure that anyone else has. All I do know is that growing up, I always felt different. An outcast. A deviant, not necessarily because of what I had done, but because of where I'd come from. Because of who I'd come from.

I felt soiled. Both in my body and my name. I was never sure if I'd ever be clean. Physically or emotionally. I remember serving Mass when I was maybe twelve years old and watching the priest perform his duties with his clean pink hands, wondering if my hands would ever be that clean, that pink. No matter how hard I tried, I was always on the outside looking in. I was not like other people.

Simply put, I felt alone.

But I wasn't. I had family and friends who cared for me. Who listened to me. Who guided me. It took me a long time to hear them and to fully appreciate them. As you read this, you know who you are. There are a lot of people reading this who no doubt tried to extricate my mother from the iron grip this man had on her and, for obvious reasons, were not successful. This was the 1970s, when divorce was frowned upon. A woman had to love and obey her husband through sickness and health—through good times and bad. Well, there was more sickness than health and more bad times than good. There is no doubt in my mind that a man wrote those vows, and that man should suffer eternal damnation for all of the women who followed this vow rather than escape the torturous marriages they were trapped in.

While I felt alone in my pain, there were others in my group of friends who were experiencing the exact same feelings. They, like me, possibly like you, just did not share that feeling of being alone with others.

It took me years to realize this, so I say this to whoever will listen: "You are not alone." Say it to yourself, and believe it. In fact, don't just say it, shout it. There is so much power in that statement. So much power. Personal power. The power to change a life. Yours, maybe your siblings', maybe—more importantly—your children's. You can and should reach out for help. Even just to talk. Or to listen.

There are others out there experiencing the same things you have or are currently going through. Maybe you live in a steamy apartment in a large city or in a noisy townhouse in a small city. Possibly you live in a trailer in no city at all. Or, you might be the one who lives in that dream house in the suburbs with the four bedrooms and a white picket fence and a family to match. It doesn't matter. We are all the same. No matter what skin tone, creed, sexuality, we all bleed the same colour, all feel the same pain. We all, at one point, feel alone. So, just don't. There is a survivors' network out there. We all just need to recognize it, talk about it and embrace it. Don't hide from your past. Face it head-on—accept and own it. Then and only then can you control it. I don't always practise what I preach, so please forgive me my shortcomings and setbacks. These things are often easier said, or written, than done.

I have to be clear: this is not meant to be a self-help book— no, this is just a recounting of the life experience of someone I'm not sure I even recognize as I look back.

I expect that it is common with many abused persons that they detach themselves from the actual experience in order to cope with the aftermath. They don't recognize their former selves. That crying child, it's not me—it's only a shadow of some poor soul, left behind by a nuclear blast. Not exactly a reflection of who I was, but an image I can only recall through blurred vision.

I guess it's a method of survival. Anyone with more education than me can qualify and/or explain this. But, as a survivor, I can tell you that is what it is. Once you are removed from the pain, the pain cannot hurt you anymore. I may be better at this than most. I can be cold. Described by some at times as a prick. Sure. I get it. I am. I've been awful to those I care about. My kids and wife can confirm this. Sometimes when there is a family crisis (and there have been more than a few), I act like a robot. When Angèle and Eric come to me with a problem, I look at the problem like a flow chart. I do try to understand the human element, but I am constantly drawn back to logic, and the path I follow in giving my advice is not nuanced with emotion, it is black-and-white.

I often deal with issues the way a programmer deals with a virus. I see in binary. Not quite 0s and 1s like *The Matrix*, but not far off. There are days when I don't even feel human. I don't cry at funerals. I've watched at least four people I loved dearly die in a hospital bed and did not shed one single tear. I'm sorry, but sometimes a person doesn't have the luxury of feelings.

Crazy, right? Feelings are a luxury?

There are some of you reading this right now who have experienced this. Who *are* experiencing this. You know who you are. It's okay. And it's not your fault.

You too, are victims of spousal, physical, sexual or mental abuse. And in far too many cases, victims of all four. Is it odd to see a man not only write about this but to admit he has experienced and survived three of the four? Twenty years ago, this may have been unusual, but thankfully we are evolving to a place where men and women are stepping out of the shadows and saying, "Me too." I would be remiss if I did not mention the importance of the Me Too movement against sexual abuse and harassment started by Tarana Burke. When that movement made headlines, I did not add my voice as this is my cross to bear. These are my scars, and for the present time, I'll cover them up and only reveal them when I am ready. Or maybe I won't. That is my right. I've kept my feelings to myself, admitting some of my past experiences to very few, and in some instances to no one.

Feelings are like the water being held back by a dam, and some dams hold back more water than others. Some let through a little water most days, and others hold it all in. Other dams divert the water. In cases like mine, I like to think that I control the dam and the flow of emotion.

Some days I'm good at it; on other days, the whole thing just blows apart. The tiniest leak can have catastrophic results, flooding an entire valley.

Hate. Love. Joy. All of it. You never know what you're going to get. I suppose that may be why some emotionally explosive people seem the most reserved on the surface. Then one day the dam either spills over or bursts, and they become a riptide, pulling an unsuspecting swimmer into the cold deep with them.

Maybe that's what happened to you, Dad. Maybe your dam burst, but the riptide you created wasn't strong enough to pull us all under with you. I do believe that at one point in your life you did try to drag us all down. At the end, you may have had only strength enough to sink to the bottom on your own.

Is this the end of the book then? Is this the answer I've been chasing? Probably not. I've still got questions.

Will I get answers?

Not from you, Dad. But asking the questions may in fact be more therapeutic than making up a conversation between a fictitious version of me and a very dead you.

LOVE?

Did you ever love us? Did you ever love anyone? Were you capable of love at all? Did you feel that anyone ever loved you? Did you know what love meant? Not in the animalistic way that most men of your generation saw it, but real unconditional love. How about conditional love? Love of any sort?

While my memory of you lasts for only seven, maybe eight years, I do have a recollection of watching you interact with others. Did I witness love? I'm not sure that I ever saw you love my mother. I cannot recall you ever saying anything nice to her. You would complain about the dinners she prepared. You would tell her that you'd be better off if you could chop her up and sell her by the pound, making reference to her weight.

That was certainly not love.

I watched you hit her, spin her around by the hair and throw her to the ground.

In Sudbury, I sat in the back of our station wagon and watched you drive by my mother as she walked those cold snowy Northern Ontario streets on her way to the welfare office. You had all of us kids in the warm car and kept driving by her over and over again and would not pick her up or offer her a ride. Love?

I know you threw her down the stairs when we lived at that farmhouse in Barryvale. She was in the hospital for a week. You had to make meals for us. What could she possibly have done to make you throw her down the stairs? The runny scrambled eggs with cabbage or lettuce that you made us one night tasted as bad back then as they sound today. I'm not sure what you were thinking there. Maybe you weren't.

How in the hell were you not arrested for that? I know it was the early '70s, but that is some serious shit. I guess while I'm writing this, I should have some questions for others, people who could have either made sure you were put in jail or at the very least made sure that you never did this to my mother again. Not only did you have your immediate family living in fear, you may have had everyone else in our small universe afraid of you too.

Jesus—were you really that tough? Men and women walked in fear—of you? Is that really the way it was, and did you like that? Were people only nice to you because they feared you? What the hell kind of life is that? Maybe that's why you felt so lonely. Maybe that's why you decided to end things, alone and drunk in a trailer.

Did anyone really like you? Yes, I've asked a few of your hangers-on about you throughout my adult life . . .

They all say the same thing: you were a great guy. I am always left in disbelief when they tell me this. What movie were they watching? It was certainly not the one I was acting in. Even if you could possibly take the abusive behaviour out of the plot, you're still left with a selfish alcoholic who could not—no, would not—keep a job in order to feed, house and clothe his family. Almost every action you took in your short life led to your own self-gratification. Whether it was drinking, womanizing, coming in at all hours and then over-sleeping your alarm clock or taking off for days at a time. All of it. Self-centred, self-destructive behaviour, with no thought at all to the impact it would have on your five kids and wife at home.

That's the problem with self-destructive behaviour. It's not really self-destructive, it's just destructive. Somewhere, somehow, it impacts somebody else. Addicts of all shapes and sizes—alcohol, drugs, gambling, shopping, whatever—have an impact on someone else. Even if you live alone, in a one-bedroom basement apartment or a mobile home, your behaviour will at one point in time cause another human being to experience something that they otherwise would not. Maybe your rent is unpaid, and the landlord ends up losing his or her building. Maybe you spend grocery money at the bar buying drinks for all of your buddies, playing the big shot, and your kids don't eat. Maybe you get behind the wheel of your car after a night of drinking or drugs, and you kill someone on their way home from working a night shift. The behaviour is simply destructive.

They say for every action, there is an equal and opposite reaction. I can tell you that the reaction is not always equal, nor opposite. A man's "self-destructive behaviour" can lead to others' "self-destructive behaviour"—equal, but not opposite. Take me, for example. I watched you abuse alcohol for years and then started abusing it myself at a pretty early age. By the time I was fifteen, I was drinking heavily every weekend, and in the summer months, most nights. I was not alone. Most of my friends were doing the very same thing.

We grew up in a small Eastern Ontario village, and most of my peers and I were binge-drinking by the time we entered high school. When I look back, most of us had some sort of similar circumstance, an addict in the family of one sort or another, and there we were, at pit parties, listening to Van Halen and drinking our brains out. Each one of us just trying to quiet a voice or erase an experience. Make the nightmares go away. Get groping hands off of us. Forget the two a.m. fist fights between our parents. We self-medicated for at least those four years of high school and, for some of us, throughout our adult lives.

If I'm to be totally honest, and I said I would be when I started this, I know there are times when I still drink too much. Certainly, there have been times in the past when I know I drank way too much. I cannot blame this entirely on you or the impact you had on me. That wouldn't be fair, nor would it address the issues I've had personally and professionally. It could also be genetic, and that's not entirely your fault either. You didn't choose which tree you dropped out of, any more than I did. The pattern, however, was set in motion, and the results of your destructive behaviour are still being felt forty years after your death. You have five children who are haunted not only by your behaviour, but by your memory. That's right, we're haunted. We've all had nightmares starring you, each and every one of us. You created a pretty big wake in a very small river. Thank God for our mother, because if not for her protecting the shoreline when we were younger, the riverbanks would have eroded by now.

So, again, to my point about this behaviour of yours being self-destructive, it wasn't. It was just destructive.

But back to the question at hand: love. I do believe, oddly enough, that you loved me. I'm not sure why, but I think you did spend more time with me than you did with my brother or sisters. I was your "little man." That's what you used to call me. Endearing, wasn't it?

It really was.

You know I've never called my son "my little man." I don't know if it was intentional or not, but I'm pretty sure that somewhere in the back of my mind, I decided not to do that. He is my boy. My son. My buddies and I have called him Jimmy since he was two and wandering around our hockey dressing room after a game. I'm proud of the nickname, and thankful for my teammates for coming up with it.

Dad, I remember one night in particular, we were living in the yellow house on the hill, next to the public school, and you had a bunch of your buddies over, smoking and drinking around the kitchen table. I was maybe three, and I woke up because, as usual, I had wet the bed. I came downstairs wearing only a tee-shirt, and I wanted to sit with the men. You didn't send me away. You picked me up in your strong arms and sat me on your knee. I was part of the group. One of the men. You know—it's a good memory for me. You welcomed me to the table, and I felt part of your group. I had feelings of being ashamed because I was not wearing any pants, but you never let on, and no one else did either. It's an odd memory, but one of the few pleasant ones. I wonder how many of those men who were sitting around the table that night are still alive and might recall this event. What do you have to say about it? What do you have to say about my dad now that you are reading this?

I know one thing for sure, Dad: I loved you. That is a fact. No matter how abusive you were, I loved you. You taught me how to pray, you taught me that it took a bigger man to walk away from a fight than to finish it. You never practised this rule, nor have I, unfortunately. When you and Mom split up in Sudbury, you held me in your arms while the town cop told Mom that I could go with whoever I wanted to be with. I chose you over her. I stayed with you while my brother and sisters went with Mom. Maybe that is why she has some resentment for me, to this day. I can't blame her. Odd, isn't it? I had seen the destruction left behind after the two of you fought—flour or sugar all over the floor, furniture overturned, and still I chose to stay with you. I spent nights on the couch while you went to bars, met and brought home women, and still, I wanted to be with you. Of course, I was five, maybe six years old and couldn't totally comprehend what was going on, but you were my dad, my rock. I've never felt safer than when I was with you.

Analyze this all you want, but I don't believe this is unusual.

Mom, I'm sorry. I know you will read this and say there is no resentment. I can't imagine how there is not, nor how heartbroken you must have been when this man held your young son in his arms and let the police tell you that the abuser in the relationship was keeping him. A son for whom you took beating after beating to protect. A son you cooked and cleaned for, who you just wanted to be safe. Your pain and confusion must have been almost too much to bear. Please let the fifty-one-year-old me apologize for the five- or six-year-old me. He was young and didn't fully understand. It was not a reflection upon you, it was a decision made by an immature, influenced mind.

Dad, did you really keep me with you during this time because you loved me, or did you do it to hurt Mom? I'm guessing the latter. You had no interest in watching over me as I've noted, you left a five- or six-year-old at home, unattended, sleeping while you went out and picked up women. I vividly remember being awakened in the middle of the night when you walked one of these women out the door as I lay on the living room couch.

The real kicker to this entire drama at that time is that you and I were on one side of a semi-detached house while Mom and the other kids were right next door staying with the neighbours. That's nerve.

Because love is such a powerful emotion I'll stick with it for a while and ask about your relationship with *your* father. It is important to note that I did not state that love is the *most* powerful emotion, as so many songs and poems would have you believe. Because that's just not true. The world has been exponentially changed more because of hatred, greed, bigotry and jealousy. Much of the damage you did to our family was because of these things. They are all related, however: love, jealousy, greed, bigotry, hatred. We are a complicated animal.

So, Dad, did you love me? Did you love us—as a group—as a family unit? Did you love my mother, your wife? Did you ever love her? What caused the split? Was it the five mouths you had to feed? The responsibilities that most men face that caused you to behave the way you did? I cannot imagine the stress that may have caused you, but I cannot imagine walking away from such an obligation. To have a family is such a gift. I am so sorry that you apparently did not see us as that. No, you seemed to see us as a burden. A burden that you created. It's like you were on a hike in the woods and kept picking up precious stones and putting them in your backpack. Once the backpack got too heavy you somehow never considered reducing the weight by removing certain objects, you just got frustrated by this heavy burden and threw it all—without any consideration for what you had collected, nor for the vessel you put them in. In your mind it may have been easier to start the hike over completely unburdened.

Dad, I focused my entire life around getting married and growing a family. I am so grateful for Suzie, Angèle and Eric. We are not a perfect family. We have moments when we argue and fight, but we're a family. I know I don't always say or do the right thing with Suzie or the kids, but I know they love me, and I love them. From a psychological perspective, I know that I have been chasing this "ideal" family unit since I was probably twelve years old and as a fifty-one-year-old husband and father realize that there is no "ideal" family unit. There is only a family unit. The entire *Leave It to Beaver* dream is just that—a dream. However, I'm so proud of my Suzie, Angèle and Eric. We have been through very difficult times together. We do not always agree. But we do our best and we do it together. We face the good times and the bad times together. We've shed a lot of tears during this crazy journey, but that is what it is—a journey. The destination is unknown. But we are doing it together, and at the end of the day, that may in fact be what I was chasing. What were you chasing? Maybe, more importantly, what was chasing you? What impact did your father have on you? What questions would you have for him, if either of you were still alive?

Your father was an odd man, to say the least. He was abusive, physically, mentally and sexually. I can state with confidence that I've witnessed all three. I know this statement to be one hundred percent true. I expect that you knew this as well. He was, after all, your father. You hated him—but did you ever love him? What power did that evil little man have over you that allowed him access to your children? You must have known what he was capable of . . . What I'm sure he did to you and your siblings during your childhood, I cannot imagine. Yet you allowed him to spend time around us. Jesus, of all the reckless things you did with us, this may have been the most careless.

The man was a predator, and he may have been more abusive than you. Did you love him the way I loved you? Did he have the same power over you that you had over me? It gives me chills as I write this to think that at some point in time I might have chosen to expose my children to you. I'd like to think that I would not have. Thankfully, I'll never be faced with that decision.

You used to take us to his place often after we moved back to Renfrew. You and him, sitting at the kitchen table, drinking; us kids, more often than not sitting in the car, waiting. There was one night when we were "lucky" enough to be invited into the kitchen. Our cousins were there, and we all wanted to go for ice cream. You challenged my brother: "If you can make my nose bleed, I'll take you all to Dairy Queen." Ice cream was a treat we got maybe once a year, but still my brother declined the request. I did not. I crawled across that table, a seven-year-old boy, and punched you square in the face, making your nose bleed all over. Just for an ice cream cone.

What a scene. Was I a hero in the eyes of the other kids because we were going to Dairy Queen? Or was I a monster for punching my own father in the face? You know, I've never spoken to any one of them about this. I don't really speak with my cousins on your side of the family. Sure, a few of us are friends on Facebook, but this has never come up. Not even within my own family. Is it a repressed memory, or is it something we'd rather not talk about? Would any of them even recall this event? I know I have. It shaped me, Dad. It affected me, Dad.

I'll never forget that moment: a seven-year-old striking his father in exchange for a treat. What kind of a lesson were you trying to teach my brother? What kind of lesson were you trying to teach me? What lesson did I learn? I really don't know. I have more feelings as an adult looking back at that scene than I did as a child living it. I don't believe that punch affected me at the time any more than it did you. I cannot imagine how it affected my brother, sisters or cousins who witnessed it.

Did you see in me at that point in time a prodigy? Someone who would take your place as the toughest man in town? Did you think my brother a coward? I'm sure you did. The crazy thing is that he was not the coward. You were. He was the only real man in the room. I'll never forgive you for what you did to him, for what you made me do to him, or for how my actions must have made him feel. In fact, maybe I'll never forgive that seven-year-old version of myself for what he did to him. The whole goddamn thing was wrong, Dad. You. Me. The entire bloody mess was just . . . wrong.

So, what have I learned about love?

Your heart will be broken at least once. And it will be okay. Seriously. Love your partner. Love your children. Love your job. Love your hobby. Just love something. Every one of these can and will break your heart. I have had my heart broken by each one at some point in time, and I'm sure I've broken the hearts of each one. This is life.

You know the old saying where it is better to have loved and lost than to never have loved at all? It's painfully true. But this experience is not free: nothing is. In order to experience real love, you must also experience loss, anger, jealousy and even hate. I'm not sure that a person can feel any one of these without having also felt love. Sure, there are people out there, sociopaths, psychopaths, who really don't experience any of these. I expect that is what makes them so twisted. Serial killers don't hate their victims—hell, they don't even know them. I believe they kill, maim or rob because of a complete void of this variety-pack of emotions. They cannot feel hate for their victims, nor can they feel compassion.

If you can hate, you can love; it's that simple. The emotions are really only one tick away on the scale of feeling. Both powerful, destructive at times, but both necessary.

Now, just because you feel an emotion, that does not mean you need to act on it. Controlling one's emotions is the most powerful gift and curse that we have. We all experience a loss of control, whether it is a night of passion or a moment of lashing out at a family member or co-worker.

But this is not about hate, or controlling my emotions, this is about love and the lessons learned. I'm still learning, by the way, which is a great thing. Once again, the great gift of being human. A person never stops having experiences or learning life's lessons.

Very early on, I chose to love rather than to hate. That is not to say that there aren't times when I get angry or lose my temper. It's just that I'm learning every day that those reactions are not conducive to healthy relationships, and while these reactions still happen, they occur less frequently.

Throughout my life, I've often reflected on something that changed my life, and it helps keep me on solid ground to this day. In 1927, Max Ehrmann published "Desiderata." The words ring as true today as they did prior to the Great Depression.

> Be yourself.
> Especially do not feign affection.
> Neither be cynical about love;
> for in the face of all aridity and disenchantment,
> it is as perennial as the grass.

DESIDERATA

I've read "Desiderata" thousands of times and always try to break down each line as its own independent statement or thought. This process has helped me think and rethink each word.

I then choose to see how each line applies to me in my current situation at that point in my life. Clearly, this is a moving target. I am not in the same situation personally, professionally or financially that I was when I was in high school when this poem was first given to me by my grandmother. Similarly, I was not in the same situation in college or when I got my first job. This is why I kept this poem pinned over my desk until I was in my late thirties. I've since handed it off to my daughter who then handed it off to my son. I am proud that it is pinned over his desk as it was over mine. I only hope he reads it and it offers the same assurances to him that it did to me.

The first line is easy . . . I mean, I am who I am, right? Maybe? Maybe not. I know I spent a lot of time being who I thought everyone wanted me to be. Sometimes, even as a man entering my fifties, I still do. I try to fit in, act a certain way so as to not look out of place. Not colouring outside the lines. Playing in the sandbox, sharing all the toys with the others. I spent many years trying to be someone else, being pretty much invisible in high school. Not wanting unwanted attention. I laughed at that sentence as I wrote it because it seems to not make much sense. But it makes perfect sense to me. There are better ways, grammatically, to make that statement, but as promised, I'm being as honest as I can, and these turns of phrase will rear their ugly head from time to time because they're real.

One of the many reasons I'm writing this is to reach others who were and are in the same situation. From young teens to adults who have suffered and are either in the middle of surviving or have survived some form of abuse. I think this is even more important today than ever, especially for younger people. At least when I was a teen I could step away from a person who was physically or mentally abusing me. Our kids today are so connected to their electronic devices, they are tethered to their abusers by social media. It's like that person is sitting in the room with them 24/7, hurling insults. The only way to escape it would be to shut off the damn phone. Well, that's not going to happen, so hopefully, I can offer some sort of assurance that there is a way to find peace.

This same device that tethers you to a bully also tethers you to millions of people who have suffered and survived abuse. It shows you possibility: you can survive, you can come out the other end of this crazy amusement park ride a better, more confident person.

Look, I'm not trying to preach. I am far from one hundred percent mentally healthy. I've made it clear: I have good days and bad days. But when I'm having a bad day, I try to stop those negative thoughts from entering my mind and think of the positives in my life. It may be something as simple as allowing myself to be proud of a project I'm working on. It's a trick I've used since I was very young. Celebrate your accomplishments, because these victories are what will bring you through the dark days and nights. Remember that they are your victories, and you own them. If you are going to allow your failures to enter into your mind, then let your wins also enter and allow them to fight it out with the losses. By doing this you are at least leveling the playing field in the battle for happiness. Root for the home team and you can be on the winning team in this game of self-satisfaction.

Pretty pie in the sky, right? If you are feeling badly, think of something positive and all your troubles will go away . . . I know it's not that easy, but I also know if you work at this consistently that it does work.

When I was a teen I tried to explain this to a relative of mine and was rewarded with the words, "I'll be so happy when those rose-coloured glasses are knocked off your face." I can't say that it hasn't happened, but every time those rose-coloured glasses were knocked off, I've picked them up, wiped them clean and put them back on. I still see the world this way. Am I an optimist? I guess. Maybe I'm just a fool. Either way, trying to stay positive has worked well for me.

I'll tell you a story. I was around eleven or twelve years old and in the basement of our house in Renfrew. My brother and I shared the basement as our bedroom. It was unfinished and at night terrifying to me, but that is not the point.

I was alone one day in the basement and as angry as I have ever been. I still do not know at what—which shows you how unimportant and useless anger really is—and I was having a major tantrum. I was crying and throwing things. In this rage, I picked up an album that I really loved and hurled it at the bare concrete wall. The record burst into a thousand pieces. I stopped when I realized what I had done. I stared at that shattered vinyl and thought: "I just broke something I loved because I was pissed off at somebody else. How does this make sense? Who did I hurt?" The answer, of course, was me.

What a revelation.

It was at that moment in time that my outlook changed forever. I realized that I controlled my reaction to a situation, and that it was either going to have positive or negative results, but those results were on me. Again, I've not always tapped into this knowledge, but for the most part I've tried to control how I react to things. An uncontrolled reaction leads to unpredictable results. Have I lost my temper and said or done things since that I've immediately regretted? Absolutely. I do, however, try to acknowledge my behaviour and correct it as quickly as possible. And secondly, maybe more importantly, I forgive myself for being human and making mistakes. This is critical to the pursuit of happiness and peace.

I am human. You are human. We are going to make mistakes. Write this down, underline it and highlight it and, more importantly, believe it. This is life. None of us are perfect. Do not beat yourself up forever over an indiscretion or action that was ill-advised. Admit and own the behaviour as something you regret, make amends with whomever you may have hurt and move on. Learn from the experience and work toward making better decisions in the future. God knows I've made many, many mistakes and hurt the people closest to me. Those I've hurt are, unfortunately, too numerous to mention. All that I can do is apologize and ask for forgiveness and understanding. I've had to forgive myself in order to move on and become a better man. A better husband. A better father. A better employee. A better employer. Some days I succeed. If I dwell on the days I do not, I will never grow into the man I aspire to be. It's the same for all of us.

We must recognize the days where we failed to live up to our expectations and make the changes in our behaviour to ensure that in the future we do live up to expectations. Not the expectations of others, but our own. This is not to say that we should not strive to meet the expectations of our parents, partners, siblings, children, teachers or employers, but to state that we should work toward aligning those expectations so that they are not just reasonable but attainable. If we are in a relationship in which the expectations are unreasonable or not aligned, it is likely time to change the relationship.

This does not apply to such things as being at school or work on time or not abusing drugs or alcohol or cheating on a spouse or partner: these are all reasonable expectations. Either you stop these behaviours or the decision to end the relationship will be made for you, usually by the other party.

Another honest admission: I am terrified about what the fallout from writing like this might be because I am not sure how those who think they know me will react to my confessions and also how those in my universe, but not my world, will view me after they read this. I am an executive at a firm with around fifty people who report directly to me. I wonder what they will think of me when they analyze my past and my present, and I wonder if this will affect my future. I've shared much of this with my boss, so I don't think these admissions will have an impact on that relationship, but this is very much like standing in the middle of my office wearing nothing but a smile—maybe back to that little boy sitting on his father's lap wearing nothing but a nightshirt. Any artist or musician can attest to the fact that when you put your work on public display there is the potential for criticism. Some deserved; some, not so much.

Those close to me already know and accept me as the flawed human being I am, or they would not be around me. Those who I am not particularly close with may change their perception of me as a friend, teammate, co-worker or boss. In any case, I am compelled to continue . . . to go through with the painful inquisition of a man who cannot possibly answer for his actions.

HOPE

Did you every have any—any at all? Did you know what the word "hope" meant? Was it ever part of your thought process? Even as a child? Did you ever hope for a Christmas or birthday present? Did you hope that your father would stop beating your mother? Did you hope that one day you would have a normal family life? Did you hope that one day you'd quit drinking? That you would have a job that you would keep longer than a couple of years? Did you ever hope to earn enough money to put your kids in sports? Did you hope that your kids would turn out to be mechanics like you? Did you hope that maybe they would be fighters like you? Did you hope that your daughters would someday grow up and marry a man like you? Maybe, just maybe, did you hope that you could stop beating my mother and that you could treat her like a human being? Did you ever hope that if you did this, that possibly, maybe, just maybe, you could forgive yourself and become a human being?

I expect that as a young man you were not hoping to get my mother pregnant—she was sixteen. Then you must have been hoping against hope that it would not happen to her again at seventeen, eighteen, twenty and twenty-one. How did that work out?

But if you did not hope for those things, what did you do to avoid it? The results tell me: nothing.

What did you hope for your first child as you held him for the first time? What about the second, third, fourth and fifth?

Did you have any hopes for any of us and, if you did, what did you do to make them come true? I'll tell you. Again: nothing. Either you had no hopes for us, or you didn't care enough about us to help us realize or appreciate our own hopes or dreams.

Maybe most parents have too many hopes for their children. Maybe we are too involved in their lives, from school to hockey to dance, or whatever we think they enjoy or are good at.

Sometimes it is too much, I'll give you that—but at least we show we care. What did you care about? Was it the mindset of your generation? Was it because you baby boomers received so little interest from your own parents that you showed little interest in the next generation? Maybe, but not in your case.

Most of my friends' parents took an interest in their kids' lives. You did not. Oddly, the only thing I can remember you showing an interest in was a bike that Barrie found in Elliot Lake. I suppose you figured that it was stolen and abandoned where Barrie found it. You took time and care to show us how to sand and paint the frame into an unrecognizable reflection of what it really was. Dad, I'll give you credit—you did an amazing job, hanging that stolen bike from the rafters in the basement, painting it matte black with white diamonds. I was, and still am, amazed at the time and care you took. It became a work of art, with its ape hanger handlebars and banana seat. I only hoped that you would have taken as much of an interest in your family as you did with that bike.

I do wonder, Dad, did you take your life because you never had hope? Or did you have hope at one time? Was it stolen from you by a pack of demons? You must have had demons. We all do. Some have more than others, and some are better at dealing with these demons than others are. The demons are more real and powerful to some than they are to others. We all fight them differently. We all have a different set of weapons. Maybe you didn't have the right set of tools; I don't know.

I know I have demons. You are one of them: probably the biggest. The most powerful, even in death. (Maybe more powerful in death.) You still have a huge influence on me. I wish it weren't true, but it is. I find myself trying to be tough when I shouldn't be.

A couple of years ago, I provoked a fight in a bar, thinking I was the toughest guy in the room. I was not. I got the shit kicked out of me. Not a proud moment at forty-seven, but even after the fight I wanted to go back and fight again. To be honest, I still do. I know—I *know*—that if I went back to that bar today, that I would fight the three or four guys who jumped me and would not stop until they were all on the ground bleeding. I believe I could do it. Whether it's true or not we will never know, because I am not you. Yes, I am almost you . . . but thankfully not you.

You know, Dad, I don't know if it's genetic or something I saw in you, but goddammit I will not be put down. I will not quit. I believe this is the same for my brother and sisters. We will not be beat by circumstance or situation. We do not know the word quit. Did you teach us that? Are we genetically designed to take punch after punch and not fall down? Each one of us has been beaten down our entire lives and yet we continue to survive. We're cockroaches, I guess. We were always "the LaPorte kids." Parents didn't want their children playing with us because we were dirty and poor. Modern-day Joads . . . without the charm.

As I've noted, each one of us survived when the entire town of Renfrew said we would not. God, I've hated that town throughout the years. The sentiment does not even make sense, but in the past I truly resented that town and almost everyone in it. I'm sorry, Renfrew—I know it's not you, it's how some of your sons and daughters treated us children that fueled my dislike of a place where my experiences were nothing short of humiliating and horrific.

I have to say, Dad, that not everyone in that town was awful. As I write this, I'm reminded of two classmates, Joyce and Diane, who almost every lunch in grade school saw fit to give me a cookie or apple that they simply could not eat because they were full. Maybe one or both of you will read this one day and know that the kindness you showed to a poor sixth-grade classmate has never been forgotten. There are angels among us. We just need to recognize them when they appear and accept their presence, grace and kindness.

But for many others in that town, who ignored us or wrote us off? You can go to hell. I'm sorry, but how many of you drove past that tent trailer in the parking lot and never thought to call child services? For Christ's sake, we lived in a parking lot for five months and no one said a goddamned thing . . .

Seriously, we were little kids with a mother not adequately equipped to handle us, and to my recollection we had not one single visit from social services. Not one. If it seems like I'm angry about this, well I am. I'm an adult now and capable of knowing just how wrong that was, even in the mid 1970s.

Where the hell was the town of Renfrew then? Who was protecting us? I know, Dad, that it wasn't *you*.

I guess this is where my disdain for the town begins. It grew as the beatings, poverty and abuse went on for the next year or so. Was anyone going to step in and save us? No, they were not. Sure, they dropped off gifts for us at Christmas when we lived out at the farm in Horton. I will never forget those men who showed up with a bag of presents, said "merry Christmas" and left. Maybe they had other families to visit, but did no one ask why they had to do this? What is going on in this home that we have to take time away from our families to go deliver gifts to these people? There was more going on than us just not getting Christmas gifts. I guess that is just the way it was back then. It was at that point in our lives that we had no hope. None at all.

My wife, Suzie, reads a lot of biographies, often written by adults who have had similar experiences, and she will sometimes say, "I can't believe how these kids were treated. How did no one step in and help?" More often than not, I'll just nod and say, "Yeah, I know." Sadly, I do know. As we grew up, there did not seem to be anyone who would help us. Yes, the Salvation Army invited us to a Christmas party where we were given a free meal of fried chicken and a toy and sent on our way back home into the arms of the very reason we were at that dinner for underprivileged children. Should we have been taken away from our parents? Well, that would not have been fair to our mother. Should our dad have been taken away from us? Hell yes. The question is, why was he not?

Suzie, you read these books where the authors recount their stories of abuse and despair and you cannot understand how these things could have happened. I'm glad for that. I am glad that most of the population cannot understand the pain and suffering that a person endures in an abusive and dysfunctional family.

This leads to the great divide in many relationships, Suzie, ours included. I'm writing this to you and to all the wives, husbands or partners of survivors of abuse. You are all in a tough spot. While acknowledging that no parent is perfect and they (we) all leave some scars on the children they (we) are raising, there are varying degrees of pain . . .

I am not trying to minimize any person's suffering at the hands of their parent or partner. We all have scars. I know that there are some who may be reading this who have suffered much more than I have, and there are some who have suffered less.

What I am trying to acknowledge is that for some of us, achieving even the most basic sense of normalcy is a success. The bar has been set so low, and even the slightest degree of acting responsibly is an improvement from where we started. I have a great friend who has had similar experiences, and we often talk about how, while we are not perfect, we are not as bad as our fathers were . . . To someone who has not experienced neglect or abuse, maybe this sounds kind of crazy. It probably is. Mainly because we are kind of crazy . . . Doctors can package this or diagnose it however they want, but for any child who grew up the way I did, it *is* crazy. The whole goddamned thing was crazy.

So, as a crazy person, self-diagnosed, I tend to measure my accomplishments in relation to where I came from. I do not live in a tent trailer by the side of a road. Success. I drink on weekends. Another success. Even when I was drinking a lot during the week, I could justify this by saying, "Well, at least I don't beat my wife or my kids. Even hungover, I go to work." Success. As you can see, the bar has been set pretty low. Even when I was not being the best I could be, I was better than where I came from. So, to Suzie and any other spouse or partner out there who does not understand the rationale for their partner's erratic behaviour, please try to understand how simple we can be. We are trying to do better than those who came before us. Now, that does not condone my behaviour or prohibit me from doing better still: I think I am. I've always been involved with my kids' sports, dance, school or whatever. The greatest joy I've had as a parent is watching my children perform. Angèle at dance and gymnastics and Eric at hockey and football. I don't know why a parent feels so proud watching their off-spring perform, but they do.

But there are moments when I'm not quite right. I know it before my family does, and they feel the effects of my moods. The effects are real. They are long-lasting and scar-ring for those around me. Angèle and Eric, I know there are moments, forever etched in your memories, when I have been a less-than-ideal father. In fact, I know that there are times when I have failed as a father. I recognized them the moment they happened: I just could not take it back. I could not rewind that moment in time and react differently. I have hurt you both. I have hurt your mother. I have hurt friends and family. As I reflect, I am proud of the fact that the only hurt I have ever inflicted was mental, not physical. Then again, which is worse? What bar am I setting for you?

I am in a position, with these words, where I can apologize to my wife and kids and to all of the spouses and children of people like me. We do our damn best, but there are days when we simply cannot hold it all together and the emotional dam bursts. Unfortunately, the effects of a man who shot himself in 1979 are still being felt today. You see, Dad, even though you never met your grandchildren, your impact is still being felt. Maybe that's not a fair statement. Maybe it is. It is just how I feel as I write this . . .

So, is there a lesson here? One of the main reasons for sharing all of this personal information is to see if I can help others who have experienced what I have experienced and to let them know they are not alone. As I was writing the previous paragraphs, reaching out to Suzie, Angèle and Eric, I realized maybe, just maybe I can try to provide some assistance to those living with survivors of abuse. But . . . that's a tough one. Most self-help books (which this is not meant to be) address the victim, not the person(s) who live (or lived) with the victim. I may be qualified to give you some insight into what could be going on in your partner's mind during those difficult days or nights. You know the days and nights: when they are sullen, detached, not saying much. Nodding absently when you are trying to engage them in conversation.

It's not that they're not interested in what you are saying, it's that they are somewhere else. Some*time* else. It really does happen. A sound, a smell, a taste can transport a person back in time. In the case of a survivor, it is often a worse place.

An Ontario fall fair, for example, should be a wonderful experience. I mean, where else on earth are the sounds, smells and sights more vivid or happy. You can smell the onions grilling on the flat top. Hear the music blasting from the rides and see the midway lights as you read this, can't you? What a great time for the entire family.

Not so much for me.

You know what you did, Dad. Maybe it was fun for you, but not for us. You would have all five kids and our mom packed in the station wagon, and you would drive by the Renfrew Fair, pointing out the lights, the sounds and the smell and tell us, "It sure would be great to go to the fair this year, if only we had the money. But we don't . . ." You would drive by over and over, knowing full well that we could also hear, see and smell all that the fair brought to that small town. Eventually we *would* go, you would pay the entrance fee, complaining about how you could not afford it, but not until after you had tortured us for what seemed like an eternity. You did have some sick sense of humour, didn't you?

To this day, I cannot go to the Renfrew Fair, and I'm reminded of it every time I take my own kids to the Ex in Toronto. What should be a great family moment for me always starts with sadness deep in my soul. We go every year now, but I fought it for a long time, and I don't think my wife or kids know why.

I'm sorry, Suzie, Angèle and Eric. It wasn't fair to you (pardon the awful, unintentional pun). It's my fault, not my dad's. I should have been a better man, earlier on. I should have battled these demons harder, rather than just find

41

excuses and bail on the family. I was, and still am at times, weak and fragile. It may be scary to hear that your dad is weak and fragile, but the truth is, we all are. What I need to work on is facing these demons head-on and trying to find ways to acknowledge them. Once I do that, and I have in many cases, I can tackle them.

This is hard on not only the survivor, but on the survivor's family. So, to the families of survivors, I ask for patience and understanding. We are hurting, but so are you. This is often not recognized, and it should be. We hurt you not only by our actions or inactions but also when you have to sit back and watch us, at times, attack ourselves through our behaviour. It's just not right. It really isn't. It should not be your cross to bear.

But it is.

When you married us, or agreed to live with us, you co-signed a loan, and you didn't totally understand how painful and long-term the interest payments would be. You cannot possibly understand just what is going through our minds. You cannot and should not understand how we can appear so successful or happy on the outside but so tortured on the inside. You do not see why we appear to not care for ourselves.

We drink too much. We smoke too much. We do drugs. We do not eat properly. We do not get enough sleep or exercise. We do not visit the doctor when we should. There are a thousand things that a person who feels like me should do and does not do, simply because we feel like we are not worthy. And even if we do these things, we wonder if it matters. Do we deserve to be here? What would happen if we weren't? Would anybody miss us? Would the noise in our heads stop? Are we slowly killing ourselves just to ease the pain?

People like us don't feel deserving of the simple things that most take for granted. I cannot believe that I live in a house like I do, drive a truck like I do or even have friends and family like I do. Crazy as it sounds and as hard as I work, I don't even believe that I deserve the success I have. I get completely embarrassed when people praise me. I do not feel worthy.

This is a serious issue as some of us actually do things to take away from our success, either consciously or subconsciously. We can't help it. We sabotage our own efforts. I know because I've done it. I know because I've talked with others who've done it. Jesus, this is so hard to explain to anyone who feels they have a "right" to success or riches. In acknowledging this, I hope that I can begin to appreciate any successes that I may have and that anyone reading this can do the same.

As an abused person, I remind myself that we do not always use a razor blade to cut ourselves.

What do I mean? Well, to be honest, I'm older than I ever thought I'd be. As a child, I could never imagine myself as an adult. I truly believed I'd be dead around the same age my father was when he died. Am I on borrowed time? Do I have some sort of death wish? Am I afraid of dying? Why is it that the two professions that I signed up for have me working at risk? If someone out there has the answers to this, I guess I'd take the advice. Am I self-destructive and—accordingly, by the nature of my previous definition—destructive? Possibly. Probably.

It is important for me to make it clear that while I'm not afraid of dying, that I'm also not welcoming death. Quite the opposite, actually—and I think it's one of my most redeeming qualities. I actually try to live each day like it is my last. I love life. I have a great wife and two amazing children. Now I'm not going to blow a bunch of smoke up your ass and say that my life is all rainbows and unicorns. My wife and kids drive me as crazy as I drive them. We fight, we struggle with bills and at times want nothing to do with each other. That doesn't mean we don't love each other and are not grateful for every day we have together. We do and we are.

I am one of the luckiest men on the planet because of my family (extended and immediate) and my friends. For some reason my group is as large as it is diverse. So, if there is a lesson to anyone, young or old, who may have had an upbringing similar to mine, there is hope. The fact that we may have faced death and accept that death is coming doesn't mean that death is coming today. There is a lot of living to be had. Good, bad or indifferent, the choice is at some point up to you.

So, another question for you, Dad: Did you face death at an early age? I mean, what the hell happened to you that you felt the need to torment us the way you did? Christ, I wish you were here to answer that one. Because there must have been something.

Did you feel that you would live forever? Did you think you were invincible? What made you do the dangerous things you did? Drinking and driving, fighting . . . Did you know that the only thing that could kill you was . . . you?

I'd love to know, because outside of spiders and snakes, there is not much I'm afraid of. I've chased criminals down dark alleys, gun in hand, with absolutely no fear at all. I work on high-rise buildings and have walked on two-foot ledges forty-five floors above the streets of Miami, and the thought of falling never enters my mind. Brave, calculated or just stupid? I am more careful probably than I've ever been, but still, a person who has been using alcohol for years to dull the pain has to ask themselves, what value do I place on my own life? I don't want to die, but truly, as I write this, I'm not afraid of it. Is this normal? I don't think so. So, why do I feel somewhat invincible at fifty-one? I'm not. I know that. I've seen enough death in my life to know that no one lives forever. Is it the fact that I've seen so much death that I know the inevitable is coming so I look to face it head-on? Is that how you lived your life, Dad? Did you feel that you faced death every day? Was it because of something your father did to you and your family when you were young? Or did you feel like you would actually live forever? In your own mind, did you believe that even death could not catch up with you? Is that why you took your own life? Was this the only thing in the universe that you felt you controlled?

FEAR

What did you fear, Dad? Was it your father? Was it my mom? Was it success? Commitment? Family? Death? You lived your entire life as a Category 5 hurricane, and it is unfathomable to think that the path of the storm was not somewhat intentionally plotted. I know a few people who cannot succeed in pure spite of themselves. I often want to ask them the same question. I've witnessed very successful people just implode for no reason. What were they afraid of? What were you afraid of? Was it so awful that you had become or might become that dad living in a nice neigh-bourhood where lawns were trimmed properly that you had to try to run away? And when you discovered that you couldn't run away, you were so damn abusive that you would force us to run away . . . Doesn't make much sense, does it?

You didn't want us, but you didn't want anyone else to have us which was evidenced in your many death threats to us if we ever tried to leave you. I cannot even begin to imagine how tormented you must have been.

From my perspective, the topic of fear could fill an entire book. I've lived for years with nightmares of the devil chasing me. Hunting me. For as long as I can remember, the devil was going to come and take me. Maybe it would have been better than being with you. Maybe the devil was trying to rescue me from you. I don't know. My options were not great.

I don't know why the devil was so interested in me. I dreamed of the devil almost every night until I left for college. It was only then that I could sleep with the lights off. I wasn't afraid of the dark. I was afraid of what it hid.

I'll tell you about my most vivid dream—the one that recurred throughout my childhood and into adulthood . . . probably into my mid-twenties.

I was alone in some sort of motel, with a gas station located across a very wide paved parking lot. I was in a long white room with many cupboards and closet doors. The room was extremely bright. The brightness hurt my eyes. I could barely focus. I had no idea what the cupboards contained; all I know is I was scared for my life. Why? Well, the devil was chasing me. He was trying to find me for reasons known only to him.

I was peering through a window into the bright daylight and could see him slinking around an early model 1970s dark-coloured sedan that was parked at the gas pumps next to the hotel.

First, he looked in the front seat, then the back and finally the trunk. There was no one else around. Just me and him. I knew that ultimately his search would lead him to this room, and I had to find a place to hide. I began opening cupboard doors in search of one that would best hide me. I was panicked, seeing no clear way out, but kept looking until finally I opened one door and inside found something that terrifies me to this day. It was some sort of child curled up and quite still. Its skin was like tanned leather and covered in coarse dark hair. I couldn't see its face but somehow knew it was dead and that when the devil found us both I would be blamed for the demise of what I can only imagine was the devil's own child.

I always woke from this nightmare just as the devil opened the door to the room, flooding it with light and terror.

I'm not sure what this dream means. Is it possible my subconscious was showing me a reflection of my own life? Was I that dead thing lying there in that cupboard? Was I somehow trying to hide so I would not become just like you? Was I already aware at such a young age that I was not going to be like you and was afraid of what you would do when you found out that I couldn't possibly follow your dark path? Was I the one who killed that beast and displayed it as though it was a piglet in a butcher shop window?

You know, as a kid I slept with my brother every night, sometimes because there were not enough beds, but mostly because I was terrified every time I closed my eyes. There we were, two young boys, sleeping in a single bed, hugging each other every night until one of us was old enough to move away. Were we afraid of the devil? Possibly. You? Probably.

You know, when I see the devil in my mind's eye, he has the same blue-green eyes as you. He never speaks, he is just there. I can't be certain of his purpose, but I believe he is there to take me with him. The destination is unknown, but frightening, nonetheless. Again, maybe my subconscious was aware that you would have been more than happy to have me follow the same path that you took, warning me, protecting me.

To this day, even in our king size bed, I reach across to put a hand on Suzie, just so I know I'm not alone. She doesn't know why I do it, but I do. Am I still afraid of the devil? Not so much these days. Do I still wake in the middle of the night soaked in sweat from a nightmare where the devil is chasing me? You're damn straight I do.

I had one two nights ago, and, as I always do, I reached across for Suzie, but she had gone to the spare room because of my snoring. I lay there, a scared and sweaty fifty-year-old man, wanting to get out of bed and go and crawl into the spare room bed just to be near my wife. I didn't; I forced myself to not do this because even in my groggy state of mind I knew just how irrational this really was. I lay back in bed, staring into the darkness, and for the first time in my life realized what was so terrifying to me about the nightmares I've had since childhood. It wasn't the nightmare itself; it was the fear of falling back asleep and finding myself back in the exact same scenario that had just forced me to wake up shaking. It was almost like I had been transported back to my childhood bed and remembered praying to God to not let me have another nightmare. This happened almost every night . . . Can you imagine a child lying in bed, not praying for a puppy or a new bike, but just for some peace in his subconscious so he could safely escape the reality of the hell that was his real life?

Maybe you could.

So, what scared you? As tough as you were, there had to be something. Someone. Maybe it was *you*. In all fairness, you could be pretty damn scary. I can't imagine what you must have seen when you looked in the mirror. Sad, soulless, empty blue-green eyes looking back at you is what I'd guess. It must have been awful lonely, Dad.

I know I feel that way sometimes. An island: like there is no living person on the planet who even partially understands me the way that I understand me or the way I want to be understood.

I'm sure I'm not alone in this assessment. Tell me, Dad, when you looked into the mirror and stared into those vacant, endless blue-green eyes of yours, did you ever see the real you? Did it scare you? Did it make you happy? Sad? Angry? Regretful? Humble? Comforted?

I recall one night when I had been drinking more than I should have been and fell under the spell of my own blue-green eyes in the mirror of the powder room. I recall it vividly: I was hypnotized by what I saw. I put both hands on the vanity and leaned into that mirror, my face just inches away from the glass. For a short period of time, seconds, maybe minutes, I fell into my own subconscious mind and grinned straight back at me, fully knowing what I was capable of becoming. What I saw was me through your eyes. Tough, unflinching in the face of danger, never backing down from a challenge or a fight. Ready to pack up and leave if I did not like my job, wife or family. Would you be proud of me, Dad? A suburban father, raising two kids, working hard, faithful to my wife? No, you would not be proud. You were reaching to me through that mirror that became a portal from my soul to yours.

Maybe, for the first time in many years, there was a kinetic connection between you and me. What were you trying to do to me? More importantly, what was I trying to do to myself? I could see it as clear as day, all the hate and violence I was capable of, all right there in *my* blue-green eyes. Those eyes of yours. God, there is a lot of anger, jealousy, revenge and arrogance in those eyes. How many people looked into those damn eyes just before you hit them? Certainly, my mother, we kids and countless drunks in bars . . . I hate to admit it, but I liked what I saw, because what I saw was power. I stood there grinning at myself, believing at that point in time that there was no one in the world more powerful than I was. Goddamn it felt good.

Then, somehow, some way, I was jarred back to reality and punched my grinning reflection in the mirror, right in my smug face, breaking the glass, cutting my hand in the process. That didn't just feel good—it felt amazing. It felt so good because I was not just punching me in the face, I was punching you in the face one last time. There was no Dairy Queen treat this time. I finally put you on notice that I *was* a suburban dad. I was not going to succumb to the feeling of the power I had when I looked at the two of us in the mirror. I didn't give a damn whether or not you were proud of me. I was proud of myself. Proud enough to punch what I thought was your vision of me in the face. Even though this incident is embarrassing to me (trust me, I had some explaining to do—never the truth, until now), it was the moment that I began to regain control. The moment that I felt like being me was good enough for me, along with the realization that being good enough for me was, in fact, good enough for me.

Okay, that last sentence might be a bit confusing to some. And I'm sure my editors will not like it, but it is the truth. I cannot try to hide it in some artful prose. I'm just not that good. I can't try to dress up the moment that I realized I was okay with who I was with words or phrases that are not mine. That really is the point. I just didn't smash Suzie's mirror that night, I smashed the image of the person I thought I had to be.

Not very poetic, but very true.

THE CELLAR

I had actually completely forgotten about it until I heard an old interview with Chevy Chase replayed on Howard Stern's show last week. He said that his stepfather locked him in a cellar for a week as punishment for being suspended from school. He was fourteen. I was driving, listening to Stern, and was immediately brought back to that small yellow house in Calabogie. And in an instant, I was being told by you to go down to the cellar through the hatch in the floor. It was mostly dirt down there, but there was a big chunk of the Canadian Shield on one half. And dark, dirty, musty. I was frightened, but at least there was a naked bulb hanging off of one of the joists. Thankfully, I was not alone. My brother and sisters were there. I believe it was some sort of a game you were playing. (You may or may not have been drunk.) I don't fully recall, you see, because I was only three years old—maybe four. I don't think we had done anything to deserve being banished to this dungeon, but who knows. My older siblings likely remember, but I will not ask them. All I know is that if I wasn't afraid of the dark before, I was after. You shut the light off, you son of a bitch, and laughed. We could hear you through the thin floorboards, just as I'm sure you could hear us screaming to be let out. Why in the hell would a father do this to his children? My whole adult life, I've only wanted to protect my kids, yet for some reason you felt it would be a great practical joke to terrify yours. It makes no sense to me, Dad, and it never will.

CONTROL

Control is an interesting word, and an interesting topic for our discussion. While I've asked you about some other things, I think that the question of control may be the most interesting.

As someone who has witnessed abuse at home and in my work life, I see control as weighing most heavily on the scales with respect to action or inaction.

Why do I say this? Well, most abusers control their victims. Whether this is physical, mental, emotional or sexual, I believe that the driving force is in fact control. Abusers want to control their victims. Unfortunately in many cases the abuser is successful. Is this why you struggled with Mom so much? Would she not give you full control? Is this why my brother and sisters frustrated you? They wouldn't relinquish control? They are strong—so much stronger than me. I gave in to you. I bought into your power at such a young age, and they did not. Is this why you were so hard on Barrie? He stood up to you when you were abusing his mother. I just sat back and watched. Is this why you disliked my grandma Molly? She would not give you control. She was tough—much tougher than you.

I know that just before your death you had broken up with a woman you were seeing. Mom and you had been split for a few years and this woman was a sweet and loving person. I spent time at her house and with her son. He and I actually became close friends. We spent a lot of time together, and honestly, Dad, you seemed the happiest when you were with her.

Did you try to control her? Did your efforts fail? Did the breakup make you realize that you do not control the universe? Was this the ultimate humiliation? What did your friends think? Did Barry LaPorte finally lose his mojo? Jesus Christ, Dad, did you have even one ounce of humility in your body? How did you not realize that what you were doing—pushing people like her away—was wrong? Pushing people like us, your own flesh and blood away? Or maybe you were not pushing us away but throwing us away. Like garbage. That is certainly how it felt. We were garbage. Disposable. Replaceable with another family. Another family you could control.

You know you tried this with another family. Actually, not another family—because they were related to us. Out of respect to the children of that family, I will not describe them further. It was not their choice to be involved with you any more than it was mine. I suspect they have their own issues with their upbringing, their own crosses to bear.

You and your new woman picked me and my brother up from school to have a talk. I was actually excited that you were picking us up at lunch hour because that usually meant that I would be having a hot lunch at the King Burger in Renfrew. Not Burger King. The King Burger was and still is a hot spot for lunch and dinner in town. It is a drive-through and to this day is my favourite guilty pleasure. Bad memories aside, Odie, you make a great burger but even better crinkle fries and gravy . . .

Anyway, you picked Barrie and me up from school to tell us something very important. We did not go to the King Burger. You drove us to our old tent trailer (could there be more of a reason for me not to want a tent trailer in my adult life?), which was parked on the lawn of one of your buddies, and you and the woman you were now seeing sat at a table and explained to an eight-year-old (me) and a twelve-year-old (my brother) that you two were in love. My brother and I sat there, confused and disappointed.

I reached into the plastic bread bag that contained a breadcrumb-covered hard-boiled egg and listened in dis-belief. I am not sure what was more disappointing. My father pulling me out of school to tell me he was in love with a relative of mine, or that I was eating a breadcrumb-covered hard-boiled egg for lunch instead of going to the King Burger.

I know it seems silly now, but honestly, with all of the shit I had seen in my eight years of being on this crazy green-and-blue marble, the lack of a visit to the King Burger was probably, at that point in time, the most disappointing.

It's always strange when our family is together at Christmas or a family function and we talk about our past. Most families talk about holidays or weddings, funerals, picnics or family reunions. Not ours. Nope, when I get together with my brother and sisters, we talk about how you used to abandon us in the car while you were at our grandfather's drinking, or about the time we ran away . . . And oddly, coldly and calmly, we talk about the time you tried to kill us. At least we believe that you tried to kill us—maybe you didn't. But what cannot be debated is that you did shoot at us with one of your rifles. The girls have a better recollection of this than me, but I do remember running and hiding while shots were fired.

And you know what is most odd about it? It's no big deal. Really, it isn't. I'm not sure why; maybe because our life was such hell that a bullet to the head may actually have been an escape. Maybe I'm being a little dramatic, because we actually ran for our lives as a madman (our father) was taking shots at or near us. What the hell was going through your mind, Dad? Were you hoping to win us back by threatening to kill us? I expect that this is a primary tactic in the playbook of abusive husbands. If the family doesn't want to stay, well then make them . . . If they leave, just threaten to kill them . . . And if that doesn't work, then you actually do kill them . . . What's horrifying is this is far too true in many instances. I guess the good news is that you did not kill us, but you did do more than threaten—you actually shot at us.

Well, I guess you showed us, Dad. It was very clear that you had the power. You didn't want us, but you didn't want anyone else to have us. Not a new concept, but a potentially deadly one.

To go one step further, and to add to the profile of a man who had to control those around him, do you remember the time you shot and killed Mom's dog? I do. This dog—Dolly was her name, I think (Mom can correct me if my memory is faulty)—was a Dalmatian. A beautiful, gentle, shy, protective dog. Protective of my mom that is. You clearly did not like that. You would not put up with that, but you tolerated the dog until the time was right to send a very clear message to everyone in the family. No one would challenge your authority as the alpha. No dog, woman or child could contest this and survive.

We lived on a farm in Horton and had two dogs. One, King, you bought for me as a present for my seventh birthday —albeit a few months late. And Dolly the Dalmatian. Both dogs were out in the pasture with the cows and apparently chasing them, putting them in some sort of peril. You grabbed your rifle and decided that to protect the cows you must shoot one. It just happened that you chose to shoot the one that was most protective of my mom.

I remember watching you shoot that animal, admiring your accuracy and lack of empathy as it fell.

TRUST/TRUTH

I have to ask about trust, Dad, because this is one of my biggest issues as a married man and father.

I get the sense that you never trusted my mom. She has said as much. There are times I know that I've had these feelings toward Suzie. I know they are unfounded. I know that I felt these feelings about almost every girl I ever dated. I was afraid they were going to leave me. I was jealous when I had no reason to be. I was insecure. I want to publicly apologize to all the girls I dated and friends I've had over my lifetime for inserting my own insecure feelings into our relationships.

Dad, did you have the type of friends that I had who would stand by you no matter what? I don't think you did. I think you had drinking buddies. That was it. And if any of *you* are reading this, you contributed to this mess. I hope you know it and can remember that one point in time when you could have stepped in and did not. Kind of like that Phil Collins song, "In the Air Tonight." There are a few of you still kicking around and I know what you saw, and I know what you did . . . *Nothing*. There was a train wreck about to occur, and you did nothing to stop it. Your hands are stained with blood. You should have been made to clean my father's brains from the walls and ceiling of the trailer where he ended his life. It's the least you could have done, you selfish sons of bitches.

I had a conversation the other day with a very good friend. We talked about his relationship with his wife and the doubts he's had in the past about her commitment to their marriage. He admitted that the doubts were completely unfounded. She had done nothing to give him even the slightest amount of suspicion that she was stepping out on him, but in his mind there was reason to suspect that every time she was not with him that she was with someone else.

I wish I could say that I never had these thoughts about my own marriage, even though Suzie, like my friend's wife, has not given my mind reason to drift in this direction. My friend, like me, had a parent like you, Dad—whose actions didn't just erode my friend's confidence in relationships, they reinforced the myth that no spouse can be true.

I've addressed this earlier, but it is important to acknowledge that others have felt and are feeling the same way that I have: betrayed by someone in their developing life. Someone who should have known better. Someone who should have not instilled mistrust in their relationships.

I cannot understate the effect this has had on me, and clearly on my dear friend, or on others who have had a parent or guardian who passed the same feelings of distrust on to those in their care. Suzie can confirm that I was, in the past, a very jealous man. Yet I love this woman more than I can put into words. She is my girl. I fell in love with her the moment I saw her, and I at one point sickly felt that every man saw her the exact same way I saw her, as the most desirable woman on the planet. Now, as I've grown, I know men are attracted to her, but I also know that they do not see her the same way I see her. It's been over thirty years. I still get excited when I see her. I am fortunate that I fall in love with her every day, again and again. I know it's not perfect—she still ticks me off, and I still tick her off, probably more often than not—but the point is that she is committed to me, and I am committed to her.

That is the truth.

That is a truth.

There was a period when I did not believe this was the truth. A truth. I was always suspecting that there was some mysterious man in the shadows. I felt I was the fool, not knowing that she had a secret love. I did not want to be played for a fool. My mind had created this incredible story that between raising two kids, mostly on her own, she somehow had time to be involved with a secret mystery man—during her "downtime."

It drove me crazy. I mean, how could she do this to me? How could she find the time? Even though my subconscious was telling me this was absolutely going on, logically I could not put the pieces together. It made no sense. Until, one day, it did. I had to learn to trust what I was seeing, not what I was imagining. I have a fairly active imagination, which can lead to all sorts of problems. This is not unique to me. Clearly my friend also has a creative mind.

Because of my own history, and also because I knew him and his wife so well, I asked what he thought the truth of the matter was. He acknowledged that he knew his wife was not cheating on him, but his mind was constantly running with so many different scenarios that he couldn't ignore them.

He knew the truth, but his thoughts would not allow him to accept what was happening in his own life. I could relate: I had experienced the exact same thing. So, I recommended something very simple. At least it seemed simple to me, and it was what helped me get through my own issues: accept the fact that his wife loves him as a truth. That she is not cheating on him was the truth.

The truth? The truth is fact. Something that, maybe, you did not know before you were either taught it or researched it.

The sky, for example, *is* blue. Sure, there are reasons why it is blue, but you cannot logically debate that on a cloudless day that the sky is not blue. That is a truth. The earth is round. That is a truth. The blood that flows through our veins is red. Also, a truth. Why can we accept these as facts, know them as undisputable, but are unable to allow other undisputable facts into our brains? Why must we debate them within the walls of our own minds?

Now I'm not saying that there aren't times when we should question the motives of others, including our loved ones, but when our minds invent situations that do not exist outside of the mind itself, should we not take a moment to pause and consider the facts, the truth? Why do our minds allow us to wander down paths that have nothing to do with the truth? Is it because we secretly want it to be true?

Some will say that this is truly a reflection of our own feelings or desires. Our own devious thoughts and fantasies.

I'll argue that it is actually our own insecurities, brought on by being abandoned during our most vulnerable and formative years. If you can't trust a parent to protect and stand by you when you could barely stand yourself, how can you develop healthy dependent relationships as an adult?

Who else is supposed to love and protect you unconditionally if not a parent?

What kind of impact does this have on the young, forming mind of a child?

How does this affect your lifelong mature relationships?

I can tell you. It leads to mistrust of even the most loving, caring and dedicated people you meet as an adult. It took me many years to recognize this as a fact. More importantly as a truth.

Suzie is honest and loyal. I have acknowledged my failures as a young man: I was jealous. I'm apologizing, here, to everyone I've ever exposed to my jealousy. But I am most sorry for Suzie. She did not sign up for this. She didn't know how damaged the package she'd purchased was.

Dad, can you see what you did?

Do you have any idea how difficult it has been for me, my brother, my sisters and my mother to move on from our relationship with you?

You never trusted our mom. You used to accuse her of sleeping around. When, during her years of raising five kids on her own, did you think she had the time? How active must your mind have been. What happened in your life that made your mind create such a series of events that, as you were out drinking with your buddies, you also, somehow, believed that Mom was doing the very same things as you?

You never believed anything that we said as kids, even when we were telling the truth. In fact, I cannot recall you ever even asking us a question. Not that you would have believed our answer, but still . . .

REASSURANCE

I was really trying hard not to write today, Dad. It's the May long weekend, and I'm out back, relaxing and having a pint, listening to The Boss. Then "My Father's House" comes on. It's a great song, sad and powerful, about a man who has a dream about returning to his father's house as a child. When he does finally get there, his father holds him in his arms as he sobs. I always think of you when I hear this song because, as I've said, I've never felt as safe as when I was in your arms. I was immediately taken to thoughts of my own son. I've held him in my arms many times and loved every one of them. Even the bad times. He always came home and into my arms.

There is one time that I will always remember, and I hope he won't mind my sharing. He was on some allergy medication that affected his sleep and his moods. He was not himself, but not entirely not himself. He had an edge; he has an edge. The same edge that I have. That you had. It's not a good thing.

Anyways, he was upset at his mother and he took a swing at her. He was maybe ten or eleven years old. He did not connect. He could not possibly have hurt her. But I lost my mind. I chased him until I caught him and carried him to his bed where I held him until he calmed down. I never struck him. It took all the strength I had in me not to. Seriously. I was as mad as I've ever been at anyone in my life.

I settled down and brought him to sit with me in the sunroom of the house we were living in at the time and explained "the rage" that we both have. I had just seen it first-hand and was not proud about the fact that I had passed this on to him. I didn't know then that the medication he was on at the time was part of the problem, but I did know that what I had witnessed in him at ten or eleven years old I had witnessed years ago in you, and years later, in me.

We sat there like two men, and I cried and apologized for passing on this awful trait. I was and am so sorry for your goddamned genetics. Thankfully, I've been able to control my emotions and have never taken a swing at Suzie. I'm hoping my son will be able to do the same. In fact, I'm sure he will. He is a good man. Probably a better man than I am. He is sweet. Hard at times. Questioning probably more than he should, but he knows right from wrong, and if I have taught him to be a better man than I am, then I have done my job.

I guess the good news is that Eric tends to be more like his maternal grandfather than he is like you. He is smart, determined, stubborn, handsome and resourceful. All of which will take him wherever he wants to go in life. That choice will be his and his alone.

While I'm writing about your grandchildren, I cannot neglect Angèle. She really is something else. I've never met a woman (yes, as I write this, she is no longer my little girl but a twenty-three-year-old woman) like her. She is intelligent, beautiful, strong, independent and difficult. She is my girl. Much more like me than may be healthy, I think. She is smarter than I am, cares more than I do and has an opinion that is also hers and hers alone. This girl will do whatever she chooses. She is that good and that strong—just like her mother. So, maybe . . . not as much like me as I'd like to think.

They are both strong and independent. I'm so proud of them and so grateful I've been there for their successes. And, I suppose, more importantly, their failures. It's when your kids fall down that it's most important to be there—to pick them up, dust them off and tell them "It's okay."

I don't tell them how proud I am as often as I should, but I do ask, every day, how *their* day went. At least they know I care. I never got that from you. Not that it matters, you never cared about anyone other than yourself anyways. Your needs, your wants, your day, your next drink.

Dad, you really missed out. Your grandchildren are amazing, and you will never get to see how your DNA has created such beautiful, creative, strong, difficult people. They are awesome. All of them. Mine, Barrie's, Monique's, Sally's. Each one of them independent, productive members of society. I'm going to say here, and I'm going to say it proudly, that we broke the curse. Actually, *they* broke the curse. They each deserve credit, because while we were dealing with our own issues, they managed to go on, grow, learn and become the incredible young people they are. Our children will make it acceptable to have the last name of LaPorte. Not one of them went to school dirty or with a sugar sandwich for lunch. They were all given a clean slate by their parents, your children. The children who never had a clean slate. The children who never had anything.

BORN THIS WAY

Something that occurred over the last few weeks made me question who and what I am. I had said something in passing that affected someone in a negative way, and while that was not my intention, there were repercussions. They called me out and put some pretty tough questions to me about where I was and where I was going. It actually made me question whether I should keep writing this book, and whether I was doing more damage to myself and to those around me with it than good. I was told that in the past year, since beginning this, I've changed. I've dwelled too much on the past, I was told—and those around me do not want to hear about it. When everyone gets together on a Saturday, they just want to have a beer and not think about the past. That they do not want to look back at where they'd come from and how far they'd come as adults. I had to look back at what I'd done in the past year and conversations I'd had with very good friends and reflect to determine if I'd become the guy who brought the party down to a place no one wanted to go.

I was really down. I mean, to the point that I questioned my entire existence. My purpose. My message to those I cared most about. I was in serious trouble.

Who was I?

Who am I?

What am I?

Am I a terrible, hurtful person? Should I question every word that comes out of me? I mean, if one comment could cause this type of a mess, should I simply shut my mouth and never talk about the past again?

Did you ever experience this, Dad? Was a simple throwaway comment from you enough to cause a shit storm? Jesus, I wish you were here to answer that, because for a period of about three days I was lost. I've never needed guidance from you more. I was blindsided, totally, completely. Did you have the ability to completely change someone's outlook, to cause forty years of friendship to be thrown away over a one-minute conversation? Were your words so biting that you could impact someone's life in such a negative way that you swore to never speak in a serious manner again?

I don't know if I've yet totally accepted the fact that I have the ability to cut people with words. I guess I have done this, but I haven't completely harnessed this power. It's both a gift and a curse.

The gift is the ability to speak in such a manner to another individual to convince them to change their mind in a sales meeting. I've done this hundreds of times, mostly when a client thinks they want one thing and truly need another. Sure, they say their mind is made up, but I know through experience that what they want and what they need are two different things. Often, I am trying to convince them to spend less money on product that will actually be used, versus a product that will sit for the next ten years and never be used. By "downselling," I've earned more customers, and a greater profit, than I've lost.

The curse is another thing altogether. I've lost friends because I'm outspoken and don't necessarily engage my mind before I engage my mouth. I have to tell you, at times this has been devastating.

In this particular case I beat myself up pretty bad. There were a couple of sleepless nights and difficult days among business meetings until finally, a few days later, driving to work, I heard Lady Gaga on the radio. It wasn't "Born This Way," but hearing her voice made me think about that song.

At that moment, I realized that it wasn't me who had the problem: I am who I am. I should be able to take stock of my past and be proud of just how far I've come. I also came to realize that anyone who did not get this maybe should not be part of my future. Sure, they are a part of my past, and a big part of my past, but that is, as they say, "the past." I suppose I spent so much time looking back as I wrote this book that I kind of forgot that. Certainly I want people in my life who look to the future, but I also want people who are not afraid to look back at how far we've come. I want people in my life who are not afraid to celebrate the journey we've taken together. Whether or not they want to acknowledge this, it has been a journey. It is still.

Dissecting what was said, I realized I hadn't changed in writing this book. In fact, whether I knew it or not, I'd been writing this book for ten years. And I've always been who I've been. Maybe in the presence of certain people, I'd avoided being who I truly am, playing a role in a play that, to be honest, I didn't want to be in. Well, I'm done with that. You know, I'm fifty-one, and I'm so glad to finally come to the realization that I do not have to be someone else, that I just need to be me. Those who appreciate me get it. Those who don't appreciate me, never will. And that's okay. That's on them, not me.

Tell me, Dad, the whole time you were playing the tough guy, were you playing a part? I've seen you cry. I sat in your lap when you did. You were so sad. Not the tough guy that beat up men and women just because you could. Do you think you could have stopped beating my mom if, instead of coming home drunk and angry, buoyed by your friends' pressure, if you'd sat with her just once, held her hands and told her how you truly felt? Do you think if you sat in front of my mom and cried and told her the pain you were feeling that you might still be here?

I've done it. I've sat in front of Suzie and cried. Sure, it took me many years before I could, but there was one night when I simply couldn't hold everything in; the dam burst. Not in the way yours did, Dad. I've never struck her . . . Instead, I told her for the first time in our twenty-seven-year marriage that I was weak. I was damaged, broken. I had issues that I did not believe any other human being on the planet could comprehend. I have no idea how she was able to take this in. Honestly, I don't. She just sat there on the edge of the bed and let me talk and cry. And I did a lot of both. The crazy thing is that there was nothing that really activated this type of behaviour other than the time and place seemed right. Both kids were out of the house, and I had a vulnerable moment and just let go. I'm not proud of it, but the moment unlocked a vault of emotions that I had never shared with any other living soul. Shackles that I'd worn for my entire life were removed. I had finally become human.

I only wish that at some point, Dad, you had taken the opportunity to become human too.

While I may say things to others that make it seem like I have no governor, I am, for the most part, guarded with respect to how I really feel. These bonds do keep me from expressing my true emotions. I'm working on it. I'm not talking about being completely uncensored, but acknowledging that, with those you love, there is a place and a time to express how you feel. It is okay to feel pain, sadness, remorse and even anger. These are all normal emotions: ones that most of us keep bottled up. The result is, well, an eruption of them all.

LEADERSHIP

"Lead, follow or get out of the way."

By virtue of your being "the man" in Renfrew, I suppose you were a leader. Were you a natural? Did you have a mentor? When did you become the great leader of men, who went into bars and conquered all? Was it the lack of control at your own home that made you impress your physicality on those around you? Did you confuse leadership with power? They are not the same, you know—you can have power and not be able to lead a one car funeral. And by the same token, you can have no power and lead millions.

Was it your physical presence that put you at the top of the food chain? Or were you just that damn charismatic that everyone wanted to be near you? With you? You see, Dad, I'm trying to peel back the layers of your mind, which is pretty hard to do with someone who has been dead for four decades. Your body may be cold, but the memories I have of you are not, so hopefully I can figure some of this out.

Who led you when you were a boy? When you were a teen? At what point did you decide that you should knock the king off of the snowbank and take over the mountain? Was the succession gradual? Did you plot his demise, or did you suddenly realize that you were stronger, tougher and more of a presence and simply stab him in the chest, making him look into your blue-green eyes while he lost his place in society, watching the life go out of his own once-terrifying eyes.

How did the transition into power make you feel, Dad? Did you feel like a god every time you walked into the White House or Butson's in Renfrew and the sea of patrons parted to allow you unimpeded access to your throne at the bar? You must have been something, having just left your wife and five kids in a tent trailer parked at the side of the road, striding into the hotel and announcing your presence. Everyone knew who you were and what you were about. Was there ever a challenger to your throne? Was there someone, maybe younger, who had his eye on you? Did you know who he was? Could you stand at the bar and look at the mirror and see not only your own reflection but his? What colour were his eyes? Were they fierce, or were they cunning? What did you feel? Was it fear? Panic? Or nothing? Probably nothing. I think you would have welcomed the attack so you could inflict some pain onto someone other than a member of your own family: change is as good as a rest.

Can you look back at who had the most influence in your life? Someone who had a positive or negative impact on the direction you went as an adult. Do you know who gave you your first drink? Can you remember your first? As I write this, I can clearly recall the first time I got drunk. The person who got me the beer was not and is not a bad person. He only did what I asked him to do.

Do you remember this person as the first person you saw strike a woman? Was it your father? Because God knows that he almost killed my grandmother a number of times. Is it possible that the violence you exhibited throughout your turbulent short life was learned? Did you see your father as a leader? As the "head of the family"? Did he drill this into your minds during Sunday dinners, where he got to sit at the head of the table, took the best and biggest piece of meat and then complained that the meat was overcooked? Did you watch him, with your blue-green eyes, in envy—hoping, wishing and waiting until you were that man? Ordering your wife around the kitchen, threatening to backhand any one of your children who stepped out of line?

Or was it someone you saw at the pool hall when you were an awkward skinny teen, skipping class to watch the men? Did they talk about how tough they were at home, how they beat the shit out of their wives if a meal wasn't on the table on time or if they didn't perform in the bedroom to their liking? Probably only half of what they said was true, but you took it to heart as fact, didn't you? You thought: This is how a "man" handles his family. How a man "leads."

Whoever your mentor was, he did a hell of a job. You became the man all of those other men talked about. You probably beat the shit out of half of them as you grew from skinny teen to dangerous adult. You probably knocked them off one by one until no one would challenge you. You became the king of your castle through brute force. Those who didn't challenge you became your hangers-on. I knew them as men, if you can call them that. I still know a few. Maybe they are old men now. I know their children. Some turned out very well, so maybe after you died, they took a hard left as well. Maybe you did something good after all. Only they know.

I have to say that for whatever reason you passed leadership on to us. Your children, every one of us, are as stubborn as mules. Good, bad or indifferent, the LaPorte kids walk to the beat of their own drummer.

Each one of us, in our own way, leads both at work and in social settings. Sometimes this is a good thing—other times, not so much.

My own experience with leadership? One of my first mentors was not met in a bar or at a family gathering—and she taught me more about leadership than just about any coach I've ever had.

Miss Phillips is probably not even five feet tall, but she's a giant to me. I've never told her this. I suppose I should someday . . .

I took the heading for this chapter and much of how I live my life from a poster she had in her grade nine classroom: "Lead, follow or get out of the way."

For most of high school I chose to get out of the way. I was not a leader, not much of a follower, so I spent four years sitting on the sidelines, watching others I felt were better, stronger, smarter, richer than me participate in sports, clubs and class. I didn't feel like I belonged. I wasn't good enough to be there. I was nobody. Just an extra on the set of a movie that no one would remember by the time it went to DVD.

Now, this is important to me to point out for a variety of reasons. To many, it's crazy to think a person could feel alone in a school with almost a thousand students and staff.

Well, they never experienced what I did. What many of us did. We were not cool. We were not attractive to the opposite sex; we did not excel. There were no colleges chasing us to have us join their team, their academic program. It's not like we were nothing, because we clearly were something, otherwise the other kids would not have taken the time to stuff us in lockers (yes, that happened), step around us in the hall or give us those glances that only judgmental high school students can shoot. It's just that we didn't know what we were. I didn't know what or where I fit in. I tried, trust me. I went through my preppy phase, my Bryan Adams, white tee-shirt and blue jeans phase and none of it worked. I was ignored no matter what I did.

Of course, I was one of the lucky ones who did have a few friends, some at school and some outside of it. They are still my friends thirty years later. For that I am eternally grateful. They got me through the dark times . . . some of them still do.

I always go back to Max Ehrmann: "If you compare yourself with others, you may become vain and bitter; for always there will be greater and lesser persons than yourself."

This is a fact: life is not fair, and we are not all equals. We like to think that we should be. Get over it. There will always be someone who can throw a ball farther, someone who can read better, write better, score better on tests or is better looking. But there are also people who throw a ball worse, score worse and are not as attractive. That's life. No two people are equal, and that goes to the plus and the minus. If you spend your time dwelling on what you don't have, then you will never fully appreciate what you do have.

I can guarantee, in most cases, what you have is more than many. Think about that.

While I'm on this . . . think about those who are good-looking, athletes or scholars. They were given gifts. Yes, they work at their crafts and hone their skills, and no one will take that away from them . . . But it is as important for them to appreciate what Mr. Ehrmann was saying as it is for those who may not have as much. It's okay to reach out to a classmate who you see struggling socially or academically. You will not get leprosy. Limbs will not fall off your body if you give someone who needs a hug a hug. Trust me. It is perfectly okay to sit at the table with the kids who may not be in your group. Even though it may not be immediately appreciated, the kindness you show will be felt years after. I'm not saying you need to invite the kids you don't have a lot in common with for a sleepover, you just don't need to treat them like lepers. Put yourself in their shoes and think about what you would like someone to do or say. A word or a gesture, holding a door, giving a compliment, can change the world.

High school English to most students is torture. Not to me.

I loved to read. Still do.

This tiny Welsh woman, one of my first mentors and leaders, opened my eyes to literature and challenged me to question what exactly the authors were saying.

She introduced me to W.O. Mitchell and to John Steinbeck and many others.

Those two men taught me, through their work, that if I was writing something that it should make the reader feel something.

Hate was okay.

Sadness, perfect.

Pain, good.

(Love was also fine.)

It was all part of the experience. For someone who had experienced all of these things in real life it was an odd kind of relief to know that these great men had also seen pain and suffering.

The Grapes of Wrath, to this day, still evokes as much sadness in my heart as anything I personally endured. I was with the Joad family on that terrible trip. Smelling the bacon as they cooked over an open fire, breathing in the dust and hating the men who tried to keep them down.

I was one of them. I was not alone.

But, back to Miss Phillips.

Not all of us are leaders, so we can be followers. If we are neither, we should really just get the hell out of the way. It is so simple to me. I had to either be in charge, listen to who was in charge or get out of the game, whatever that game may be.

I took these words literally and decided that I was not a good follower and needed to improve my leadership skills.

You see, in English class she had us keep journals, and she would read them and make remarks and correct grammar (a lot, not alot).

I not only loved reading but loved writing as well. I've written pretty much since I could read. My mom saved one of my earlier attempts at writing a novel and gave it to me a few years back. It is embarrassingly awful—but hey, I tried.

I posed the question, in my journal to the one person I knew was qualified to say if I had any writing ability at all. I wrote, "I'm debating whether to apply to college for policing, or if I should take journalism . . ."

The red pen response said it all: "I'm sure you will make a very good police officer."

Was I crushed?

I don't recall.

Disappointed, likely.

Regardless, I went to college to become a cop, and it was the best decision I could have made.

God, I wish I could find that journal. I'd love to frame that one page, where the answer to a confused teen's question changed his life forever.

It was in college that I made the decision to finally act like a leader.

But who was I leading? Me, of course. Others would follow, or they would not. I had to take control of me so that I could reach my goals.

I had decided that, in order to get over my shyness, I would speak in front of the class at every opportunity. I joined the social justice club and volunteered for security at a number of events. I made the choice to not be invisible.

You see, I wasn't visible in high school, not because the other kids didn't want to see me. It was that I didn't want to be seen.

That changed once I decided that I was in fact good enough, I had every right to be there and was going to make my presence known.

I controlled the situation, rather than accepting that the situation was controlling me. I studied hard, partied when appropriate and graduated, and I met a damn good woman on the way.

All of that was possible because I refused to follow or get out of the way.

I often have this conversation with my daughter when things are not going as she'd like. She struggled being away from home for her first year of university, and I would ask her simply, "Are you controlling the situation or is the situation controlling you?"

Once we had talked through the tears and anger, she would see that only she had the ability to make the changes required so that she now controlled the situation.

Now, there are situations that are out of our hands: the death of a loved one, being laid off by an employer, catastrophes. To me, it's how we react to these situations that really determines who is in control.

When tragedy strikes, I believe we have two choices. Curl up in a ball on the floor or get the hell up, dust ourselves off, say "Dammit that hurt" and move on.

Dad, thankfully, my first mentor was not you or someone like you. It was a woman who stood barely five feet tall who let me know it was okay to be who I was destined to be . . . So, did you become the man destiny wanted you to be, or did you divert the path and become the man you wanted to be? Or the man you thought you should be? We will never know.

HUMILITY

By all accounts—Mom's included—you were smart and talented. There wasn't a machine or a vehicle that you could not understand or repair. I'm guessing this is why you had so many job opportunities. The question is, why did you need so many job opportunities? The obvious answer is that you could not hold a job. How does a man with so much apparent talent continue to be dismissed from well-paying jobs? I'm guessing any good work you did when you decided to show up was forgotten by your bosses when they weighed this against your constant tardiness or outright absences caused by the many benders you went on during a regular work week.

And that's probably part of it. Maybe most of it. But I think there may have been more than that. I think that maybe you were bored. Or scared. Likely both. For all of the negative things I've heard about you, no one ever said that you were not capable or that you were particularly lazy.

Strange that a bright, hardworking man couldn't hold a job. Surely this is not the first time in history that this has been noted. In fact, I believe that it is quite common in someone with your character traits. Intelligent and hardworking, but easily bored.

I'm not here to flatter your memory, by the way, I'm just trying to figure things out. If that means saying something nice about you, so be it. Guys like you and me get bored easily. You get a job, figure it out, think of ways to improve the job or the process and either your boss is receptive to the proposed changes or he is threatened by your ideas.

What happened when you made suggestions? How did your boss feel about your ideas? Was he threatened? So, what then? Did you continue fixing cars the way they always did, Dad? If your bosses didn't listen to your suggestions, did you get so frustrated that you told them to go fuck themselves and moved on to the next job because you knew with your skill set, ability and overconfidence that you can get a job at any garage in town?

This is important . . . because I've experienced this myself, and until I started writing this, never for one second considered that this might be why you quit or were fired.

I've left two very good well-paying jobs for this exact reason.

I was a cop for nine and a half years. I knew I was going to be a cop since I was three years old. You remember, Dad, don't you, when you and I were at the dump in Calabogie, and that OPP officer and you were speaking? You and he were outside talking about who knows what, and he asked me if I wanted to climb inside the police car. Of course I did. I sat on the driver's seat of that car and looked at all the equipment (which, by today's standards, was pretty bare) and was amazed. I knew I wanted a job where I could operate all that gear.

As I grew, I saw that the police officers in our small town of Renfrew all seemed to have pretty good lifestyles. I measured my life against those of the kids of police. They all seemed to have nice clothes, decent lunches and good hockey gear. This only reinforced my drive to become an officer—with a steady job, I could provide these kinds of luxuries for my own kids.

I worked my ass off, physically, mentally and, yes, socially, to make sure I became a cop. I had a lot of detractors. Those who would not let me forget the "LaPorte Curse." I was too small. Too weak. Too mouthy. Too poor. It was those voices that kept driving me to finish every mile, do one more push-up or sit-up and study harder for that test. I heard those voices every time I felt like quitting and just going back to Calabogie to work at the ski hill. They were with me every step of the way. To them, I say thank you: I'm not sure I could have done it if many of you had told me I could.

I kept my nose clean through high school, was the first ever co-op student at the Renfrew Police Department, paid my way through college four hours away from home and graduated scholar.

Sure, it took eight months from graduation until I got hired, but I did it. I was twenty years old and on my way to a future brighter than I could have ever imagined. I had achieved my ultimate goal in a very short period of time.

Fast-forward nine and a half years, and I had left this dream behind. Mostly for personal reasons. By leaving I got to stay married to Suzie. Things were not great between us . . . mostly, because we just didn't communicate. Or, more correctly, I did not communicate.

Being a cop is tough. Sure, everyone says that, but not everyone understands just how tough it is. You know, after a couple of years on the job, I stopped feeling badly at funerals. I had seen more dead bodies in my first four years as a cop than most people see in a lifetime. Part of my job was to photograph crime scenes, which included sudden deaths, suicides and major accidents. I suppose a man can only walk through so much blood before he stops noticing it. Dead bodies have as much meaning to a cop as dead cows to a butcher. It's just part of the job. Can you imagine what that does to a person? Naturally they want to feel some sort of grief for the deceased and for the deceased's loved ones. The problem is that if a cop becomes emotionally attached, they can't do their job properly. When emotions become involved in a cop's decision-making process, they tend to do something stupid.

The two incidents that brought me closest to crossing this line took place on the same day. I arrived for day shift as usual at five a.m. and was sitting in the parade room by five thirty. I got the call early to head to the adjacent town because a little girl had been abducted overnight and a full-on search for her abductor had been launched. This was the stuff of nightmares for parents. This did not happen in our town. This did not happen in Canada. Truly, this was the type of thing that only happened in big American cities. Regardless, I was in my car, partnered with an officer held over from the night shift and on the way to assist in the search for this monster.

As we patrolled the area where she lived, a resident of the town called in and said that he had found the man and the girl in a shed in his backyard. The chase was on. My partner was on foot, in pursuit with other officers, racing through backyards, jumping fences. I mirrored their movements in my patrol car until he was finally caught.

He was cuffed and placed in the back seat of my cruiser, and I did one of the hardest things I've ever done as a cop. I read him his rights. I had to look at this piece of human trash and let him know that he had rights. What about the rights of that little girl he had stolen in the middle of the night and then violated in some damn garden shed? She will never be the same. I'm not sure any one of us who were involved in this case will ever be the same . . .

I never knew her name, you know; I still don't. This happened twenty-five years ago. I wonder where she is now. I wonder how she is doing. Has she come to terms with what happened to her that fateful night? I wonder if she is reading this now. I hope to God she has miraculously forgotten about the whole damn thing. I wish I could.

I do know I just wanted to throttle this guy so that he would never do this type of thing ever again. Unfortunately, as an officer whose job it was to lock away the animal and protect the rest of society, I had to do the right thing and ensure he got to jail in one piece and fully understood his rights to a lawyer and a fair trial.

Well, I got him to jail and did up the appropriate paperwork and made my notes so that there would be no openings in the case for a clever defence lawyer to crawl through. I ate my lunch and was back on the road by three p.m. What a morning. The next thing I knew, I was engaged in a full pursuit with a stolen car in the south end of the city. One of our detectives in an unmarked car spotted the car and called for help. I was close by when this guy decided to make a run for it. Now I found myself racing through the streets, lights and sirens going, and this maniac would not stop. As I was travelling north, I saw that school was letting out and the sidewalks were crowded with children on their way home, so I did the only thing I could and called off the pursuit. I shut down lights and sirens and backed off. I saw the car turn on a westbound road, and I shadowed him by turning west on the first street south of him. I lost sight of the car for maybe thirty seconds and turned north on the first available street. What I saw ahead scared the hell out of me. The car had plowed into a fence of a local business. Smoke billowed from it. I raced to the scene, got out of my car and pulled the driver from the wreckage. Another officer joined me and began to rough this character up. This guy had not only hit an elderly couple's car head-on and kept going, but he'd also endangered the lives of countless school children. I wanted to hit him as bad as the other officer, but I could not allow him to give the courts any reason to let him walk. I restrained the other officer and continued with the arrest.

That was just one day in, by most standards, a small city. I can't even imagine what officers deal with in other major cities, so there is no way that the public can. It's not their fault; really, it isn't.

When there's a police shooting, it's amazing how the armchair quarterbacks question why the officer didn't just shoot the guy who had been waving the sword in the arm or leg . . . Really? Have you ever fired a pistol under normal circumstances—let alone when the adrenaline is coursing through your veins and your heart is pumping a million miles a minute—and tried to hit something five inches wide from twenty feet away? Of course you haven't. Most people never see or experience what I and other officers have seen and experienced. But that's what I signed up for.

I'm not singing the blues, just explaining one of the reasons I left the police force: I stopped talking with my wife. I could not, in good conscience, during our nightly supper conversation, talk about trying to figure out how to cut a nineteen-year-old boy who had committed suicide down from a tree while trying to preserve the knot in the belt so that we could prove it was not tied by someone else. These are the things cops have to deal with. Bad enough that you're staring a dead teenager in the face, tongue sticking out of his mouth, eyes bulging, but now you have to preserve evidence. The scene has to be maintained, uncontaminated. If you don't do your job properly, the parents, aunts, uncles, grandparents will blame you for never getting closure on their son, nephew or grandson's murder. Naturally, they are all looking to blame someone for this loss. They are grieving, and in the first stage of their grief—denial. Their son would not do this—there must be another explanation. More likely he was killed, but the cops didn't handle the crime scene well, so nobody will ever be brought to justice for it.

Even though you know he left a note.

Officers take copious notes and photographs of a scene that most people will never have to see. They carefully preserve evidence so that they can prove to someone that the deceased had done what we all knew he did: took his own life. It may be part of the job, but there are not many other jobs where you are scrutinized from the time you sign in for work in the morning until you sign off at night. Every decision a cop makes is under a magnifying glass. Not that it shouldn't be, but people really need to understand that. If you make a mistake at your job, maybe somebody receives an incorrect invoice. In the cop's world, a mistake can cause a person to lose their life. Clearly there are other professions where life hangs in the balance—doctors, ironworkers, pilots, nurses and firefighters to name a few—but this was my world, my experience.

Suzie still does not know everything I experienced during my time on the force. I had some great times, worked with great people, but also had some brutal experiences. Experiences that will stay with me for the rest of my life.

I suppose the experience that hit closest to home took place on Christmas Eve 1996. I was working the night shift, but went with Suzie to our friends' house to spend the evening. We didn't have kids yet, and she did not want to be alone.

I had barely gotten my boots off to go in for a coffee when I got the call. Suicide—go investigate and take photos. I said "Merry Christmas" to my friends and my wife, put my boots back on and headed back to work. It was a suicide, all right. A bad one. I guess they are all bad, but this scene was gruesome. A shotgun blast to the head. The deceased was sitting on his bed, back leaning on the wall, shotgun on his lap and the top of his head blown up the wall behind him, across the ceiling and back down the opposite wall and all over the floor of this small room. I can see it as clearly today as I did twenty-three years ago.

I spent a couple of hours walking on skull fragments, brains and blood, all the while thinking of you. Knowing this is how you died, Dad. Violently. Alone. Every photo I took that night was of you. I thought of you every time I felt the crunch beneath my boots. Each breath I took I inhaled the same stale smell of blood and gunpowder that would have been present after you shot yourself.

I watched the funeral directors take your lifeless body from the scene in a sterile white body bag. Then I went back to work.

I suppose I could have had someone else take the call, but that is not who I am. Not who you were. Not who we are. I knew this call was coming at some point, and I had to face it head-on. Otherwise, I would have always lived in the fear that it was coming. I'd rather just get it out of the way and place this very painful and disturbing event in a locked vault.

Healthy? Probably not.

Do I regret it? Nope.

I guess it gave me a little insight into just how lonely and despondent you were at the end. That Christmas Eve I was not in some sad bedroom in Oshawa photographing an unknown suicide victim. No, I was in a trailer in Renfrew, taking photographs of your corpse.

Merry fucking Christmas.

The point is, that for a variety of reasons, I left a very stable job. And the personal toll was only part of it. The other part? I was not being challenged as much as I'd have liked. I had supervisors who, rightly or wrongly, I felt should not have been supervising me—or anyone else for that matter. Sure, I was involved in some major investigations, which challenged me, but at the end of the day, I knew that I was not ever going to rise above the level of constable, and I was not entirely comfortable with that. As it turns out, Dad, I'm not a very good follower. I have to wonder if that was one of your issues with everyone you worked for.

Based on what I hear from your friends and family, you were a leader and likely did not take to people leading you when you felt they were unworthy.

I began working full-time for the company I'm with now, a company that I've worked with, off and on, since I was nineteen. While I was at the police department, I worked for this firm on almost every day I had off. When I finally left the police department, I went directly into sales and was managing the inspections department along with overseeing our Vancouver operations. I had responsibility and was being challenged daily to understand this industry and the people in it.

Once again, I worked my ass off, evenings and weekends and travelled to the States way more than a man with a young family should. I became the number two salesperson in a very short time, was running the most profitable division in the company and wanted more. I needed more. I submitted ideas as to how we could grow the company and be ready for new legislation that was sure to pass in the US. I felt that my recommendations were not only not being taken seriously, but that they were being ignored altogether. There is a difference. When you are not taken seriously, it means that someone actually read your recommendations or business plan and disagreed with it. When you are ignored, it means that your recommendations were just not read. As an employee, nothing is more disheartening than when your boss doesn't even consider your proposals. Lesson to any managers out there: even if you don't agree with what your employees are submitting for review, take the time to read and respond. Otherwise, they do what I did, for the second time: quit a secure, well-paying job to work for an upstart competitor.

Dad, I committed the cardinal sin: I read my own press clippings. I had a lot of people both inside and outside the firm telling me that I should be president and that I was unappreciated. If a job offer came up, I should take it. Well, I began to believe these people and thought I was bigger than the company I'd worked for since I was nineteen. I was wrong—boy, was I wrong.

I can tell you the greatest regret that I have is leaving a secure job and putting my family's welfare in jeopardy because of pride. I flew too close to the sun, and my wings melted and burned. Badly.

The choice I made had such an adverse effect on my wife and children that I'm not sure any of us will ever fully recover. I guess this is the difference between you and me. You never seemed bothered by the results of your decisions. I am. I am reminded of my choices every day as I have to look across the street at a house I used to live in. I had to sell that house because the firm I went to could not afford to pay me what they owed me. I did everything they asked me to do, tripled the business in a year and, at the end of the day, the CEO told me if they paid me what they owed me they would go bankrupt. I did not want to be responsible for other people losing their jobs.

I tried to hold on for a bit, started my own company with the buyout they gave me, but that lasted just over a year before I made the most humbling decision I've ever made in my life. I crawled back to the company I originally left.

The walk to the front door of the office that I used to work at was probably one hundred feet from where I parked. I felt every one of those steps. I had abandoned these people. They were, and thankfully still are, family.

Our building is located in a mixed industrial and residential section of the city. It was designed to look less like an office and more like a home. The brick facade has large floor-to-ceiling windows facing the street and the walkway up to the front door. The owner has a modest corner office that looks out on both the parking lot and the walkway. I had to walk past his window to meet with him to ask for a job. Not my old job, because that was gone—for any job. I was ready to sweep floors. Goddamn was that hard. With every step I took, I just pictured my wife and kids and was reminded of what I had done to them. What a fool I was, Dad. Really, there is no other way to describe it.

I walked in that front door, and Christine welcomed me like I'd never left. That took some of the pain away. Thank you, Christine—I'll never forget that moment. Then Marc, the owner of the company, saw me, and as hurt as he was by my leaving, walked up to me and gave me a big hug. Of course, he ribbed me a little about leaving, but that hug gave me something you never offered—hope.

I'm going to talk a bit about Marc here—if he doesn't want this in the book, I'll delete it, but this is important to me. It's important because Marc has had more influence on me than just about any other man in my life.

I met Marc when I was just an eighteen-year-old kid dating his family member. That family member would become my wife of thirty years. I was young and impressionable, and Marc made quite an impact. He still does, every time he and I meet and talk about business or about life.

There are two sides to Marc, both incredible. I have never met a person with more perspective on life or on business. I can recall almost every conversation I've had with him, and he has influenced me more than he will ever know. Sometimes I follow his advice—and sometimes I don't, but that doesn't mean I'm not listening.

I'll start with the business side of Marc. He works harder than anyone I know. He built his business from the ground up. I know because I saw the prototype for it when I was eighteen, and he showed up at Suzie's parents' house one Christmas or Easter for a visit and had it in the trunk of his car. He showed my now father-in-law and told him that this one item was going to change an industry. Now, at that point in time I was just a background character in a play as Marc knew me only as the guy dating a girl he'd known since she was six or seven. He did not pay much attention to me, but I paid attention to him. After Marc left, the guys were talking about how Marc always had something going on. Was always developing a product or building a business. I didn't know Marc's history, so I couldn't comment.

Fast-forward a year, and I'd graduated college and was looking for work. My brother-in-law was doing some work for Marc in Ottawa, trying to build the business, while Marc and his crew were taking Toronto by storm. There were maybe five or six total employees. Gerry offered me a job in Ottawa while I waited to get hired by a police department. I took the job, and it changed my life. Gerry, I love you like a brother and have never met a more selfless man or father. You give everything and expect nothing in return.

So, Gerry hired me, and then I spent a week in Toronto with Marc and his group training for this new and exciting business. Marc is a great mentor and a great talker. I've seen him take over rooms; actually, the truth is, when he walks into a room, people concede the room to him. He commands that kind of respect, truly. He has a vision that no one I've ever met can keep up with and understands business better than any professor at any university or college.

His company has grown to somewhere around a hundred employees, and I'm proud to be a part of that.

But there is also the personal side of Marc that is equally important, and it's pushed me to be a better father and husband. I'll reference two things, but there have been many examples.

I met Marc for a coffee one day and the subject of having kids came up. Marc, the businessman, took a bit of a pause and said that he wished he could keep his kids young forever. He began talking about how he loved spending time with them, fishing, going for coffee, little things. He wanted to keep them with him forever.

It was so heartfelt and honest that it left a major impression on me. Now this may seem strange having come from a man who spent countless hours away from his family to build his business, as have I, but I never let this moment or advice leave me. I've been a far from perfect parent, but I've been involved. When I was home, I was present, decorating Christmas trees, having Easter dinner, attending every parent meeting and countless hockey games, gymnastic competitions and dance recitals. When I was home, I tried to be home. We camped, hiked, fished and did all the things that you did not do with us, Dad. Sure, you took us camping, but then you'd disappear for three or four days with your buddies. Setting up a camp for your family is not camping with your family. I'm sure my wife and kids would say that there have been times when I've been distant or disappeared as well. I would agree. For that, I apologize, but I did the best I could. It is for this reason that I thank men like Gerry and Marc for setting the example.

The second example of Marc's influence on me is kind of strange. I may have been commenting on something Suzie did or did not do one day, and he looked at me and said, "If you have no expectations, you cannot be disappointed." He said if supper was on the table when he got home he would be appreciative, but he would not be disappointed if it was not because he did not put these expectations on his wife.

That was life-changing. Not just in terms of a marriage, but in all aspects of life. That's not to say that we shouldn't expect certain things from people in business, but in life, most of our disappointments come from our own expectations. Did you order the product when I asked, issue the shop drawings, call the plumber or clean the bathroom? You can go on and on. If you don't expect that these tasks will be done, you cannot be disappointed when they are not. That is not to say that these things won't get done, but by putting your expectations on someone else, you are setting yourself up for disappointment.

Why so much time on Marc? Well, as you can see, Dad, he has helped shape me as a man. I've only brought up a few examples of how he's taken me in, guided and mentored me. I hope he won't be embarrassed by my bringing this up, but he has been more of a father to me than you ever were.

So, what does this have to do with humility? A lot. I have accomplished a lot, but I've also lost a lot. I've hurt a lot of people in the process. I am painfully aware of the fact that my decisions affected so many in ways that I could not have imagined.

I don't think you ever did that. I don't believe you had it in you to admit defeat, to acknowledge that you had made a mistake, to humble yourself. But I had to—I was about to lose everything that I had worked so hard for. You were not afraid of losing it all, or you would not have parked your wife and five kids in a tent trailer in the parking lot of an abandoned church next to a busy highway.

I mean, Jesus, Dad, we left a beautiful, if humble, home in Elliot Late to go back to Renfrew where we lived for five months *in a parking lot*. We had no running water, plumbing or other basic services. What was it, 1975 or '76? And there we were living like it was 1875. I know many people have had it worse than us, but a tent trailer was okay for a week at Grundy Park, not for five months in a dusty parking lot.

How could you ever have thought this was a plausible solution for whatever your issues were? Did you lose your job at the mines in Elliot Lake, or did you just up and quit? Either way, I don't get it. You were sober for at least a year up there, and we were evolving into human beings. We were beginning to fit in. For a very short period of time, maybe, just maybe, there was a light at the end of the tunnel. And then, as the old saying goes, the light turned out to be a train.

I will say, that as good as things were in Elliot Lake, the LaPorte Curse had not left us. I was in grade one and pretty unaware of what was going on around me. I attended public school with my siblings and on one particular day was asked to stay behind while my classmates went for lunch recess. In that mostly empty classroom was me, my brother and my two older sisters. During our entire detention, we were grilled by the teacher asking us to confess to one or all of us stealing money from a student's desk. I hadn't stolen any money and am pretty sure none of my brother or sisters did either. As I look back on this, I completely understand pro-filing. Once again, I felt dirty. No matter how hard we tried, we could simply not wash those stains off of us.

You moved us so quickly, I don't even know what you did with our furniture. When I reflect back, it seems like we moved in a week. I remember you and Mom going down home for the long weekend in May, and then all of a sudden there we were in that black station wagon, towing the tent trailer across the Canadian Shield back to the Ottawa Valley.

Where did all of our stuff go? Did you throw it out, or did you sell it? There is only so much stuff you can jam in a tent trailer and a station wagon. Where did our toys go? School projects? Gifts? What was the value of that, and what damage do you think it inflicts on us when we look back at the low value you placed on us and our things?

I mean, I've kept cards and drawings my kids made for me since they were old enough to hold a pencil. I would have thought that you may have kept some sort of memento to remind you of the days we spent in Northern Ontario. Maybe I'm just sentimental—but I hang onto things that mean something to me.

For example, the one item that I have that you gave me is a Timex watch. You gave it to me for my First Communion. I don't know why, but Mom was mad about it. I think you two may have been split by then. Maybe her anger had nothing to do with the watch. I still have it. My son, Eric, will have it one day. It won't mean much to him, I expect, but I'll pass it on. It still works, you know, and other than my brother and sisters, it's the only real live connection that I have to you.

The second is your old blue steel tool box. I don't know how Mom got it after you died, but she had it, and Donnie (her second husband) used it for a long while and eventually gave it to me. No tools—just an empty box.

Strange because when we reference a hockey player with a lot of talent and no drive, we say he has all the tools and no tool box. You, sir, left me a Timex watch and a tool box with no tools. Armchair quarterbacks, please discuss.

I filled that thing with my own tools, and every time I grab that blue steel box from my workbench and look at the Prowler and Hot Rod stickers that you affixed to the lid with your own hands, I think of you. Not angrily, sadly or fondly—I just think of you for a moment, grab the tool I need and go to work on whatever it is I'm trying to fix.

So, what does all of this have to do with humility? I don't know if I'll ever have the answer, Dad. I really don't. But it seems like every word I write leads to another question, thought or memory, and that they're all interconnected in one way or another.

SUCCESS

I don't like to talk about my accomplishments. That is not to say that I'm not proud of things I've done, but acknowledging achievement is hard for me. I'm not sure why, but I'm actually embarrassed when I receive praise.

When I was promoted to my current position, it took me two weeks to tell my mom. She was so proud when I called her. I guess that's a typical Mom response, but even with her, I was embarrassed—I could tell on the phone that she was almost in tears.

As much as I was driven as a young man to succeed, I still go through periods where I don't feel like I deserve what I have. The house, the car, the money. I just feel like whatever I'm doing can and will be taken from me at the drop of a hat. That at some point my boss will realize that he has hired one of "the LaPorte Kids" and fire me on the spot. I have always had such a difficult time asking for a raise because asking for more money takes me right back to my childhood—getting welfare from the city—asking someone for a handout. I know that this is completely irrational because I offer good value for services rendered, but, Jesus, this feeling has never left me. Every time I go to negotiate a new pay structure, no matter how many hats I'm wearing in the company, I am transported back in time to being a little blond-haired kid holding his mother's hand in the welfare office.

Regardless of how hard I work or how much I accomplish, I don't feel like I deserve the rewards. This may be the most damaging quality I have; I know this has held me back at times. Maybe this is because of the bad decisions I've made in the past few years that affected my family in such a negative way. Maybe it is because as a child I felt completely worthless. Maybe it's a combination of the two. I can tell you that as a parent, the best quality you can leave your child with is a feeling of value.

A few weeks ago, Suzie and I were talking, and she was telling me about a Netflix series she was watching about killers who were telling their stories, and how sad she felt for this one particular admitted killer who, for his entire life, had felt worthless. God love Suzie, but she looked at me and said, "Can you imagine that feeling?" I had to take a breath, and I said "Every day" and reminded her of my past. Of course she was immediately apologetic and explained that because I had chosen a different path that she didn't see me that way. I understood, but not without a bit of sadness. I mean, I get it. I function in society and have done well for my family, but the fact remains, there are days when I feel unworthy of my success, family and standing in society. Maybe one day I'll get over it. I do hope so.

I always wanted to be successful. Ever since I was a little kid. Money, success and leadership were all part of how I envisioned my adulthood.

Strange as I look back at the young boy I was who wanted nothing but success and the adult I am struggles with it.

I'm not sure where this drive for success comes from. I like nice things. I like quality things. I have no business liking them. I did not grow up with proper sheets, clothes or anything for that matter that was considered "fine."

So, Dad, did you have an affinity for finer things? Did you prefer shoes or clothing that was more costly but lasted longer?

And what the hell does this have to do with anything?

I'll tell you. From the time I could formulate any sense of what was going on around me socially and economically, I wanted to be successful. That's difficult for someone so young. Seriously, when I look back, I was superficial and acted like I was born a Rockefeller. My poor mother—she tried to buy Christmas gifts that would satisfy me, but year in and year out she failed. Not because of anything she did wrong; because of me. I know it now, and, sadly, I knew it then. Still, I never let her off the hook. Here was this poor woman, working as a cleaning lady, making little money, raising five kids on her own, and I had the audacity to complain about Christmas presents. I was awful. I hope she forgives me, because at times, I can barely forgive myself.

So, I knew that I wanted to be successful at an early age.

I wanted nice things, Dad. I wanted what other people had. Did you?

Every time you took a new job, did you have plans for running the entire operation? I did. I can tell you why I never wrote my sergeant's exams while I was on the police force. I knew then and know now that if I was going to be promoted, I would have to have been promoted all the way to the top. This was not arrogance or overconfidence, because clearly, I had little of both. I was just not a good follower; I wanted to be the captain of every team I played on. When I did a group presentation in college, I was the lead: I couldn't help it. The best way for me to protect myself from disappointment in the police force was to just not try for promotion. As they say in police circles—both the chief and I had gone as far as we were going to go.

That is not to say that I had given up on success. I just achieved it outside of the police department. Regardless of what business I've been involved in, I've always treated the company like I owned it. I was and am driven. This does not necessarily mean financially, although that is part of it. For me it was mostly the pursuit of goals that others told me were unattainable.

I went to high school in the '80s—my role model was Michael J. Fox. First of all, he was Canadian. He was handsome and in many of his movies played the underdog who ultimately became successful. I was Alex P. Keaton in high school, without his charm. I wore ties to school. Followed politics and the stock market. I knew more about my country when I was seventeen than I do now. I loved his drive, his relationship with his "hippie" parents, all of it. I strove to be like him—I was him for a while, just without the million-dollar paycheques. He was the role model I needed at that time: someone to teach me how to act with girls, in school and in business. *The Secret of My Success* could have been my road map to the corporate world if I had not been so damn driven to be a cop. I loved and commiserated with the drive and determination of Michael J. Fox's character. I wanted what he wanted. I actually wanted to be him. I guess in our small town, I was him. Or at least I thought I was him. If you factor in the amount of time I spent stuffed in lockers or running from guys trying to stuff me in lockers, you will see that I was clearly not Michael J. Fox or even Alex P. Keaton. I guess I was more like George McFly—*before* he was cool.

I don't know what gene or thought or incident drives me, Dad. But there are times when I wish I did not possess this quality. I'm not sure if it came from you or not as your test sample is not very reliable. I know that you were often hired in positions that required you to be trusted and responsible and they all ended the same way—with you looking for another job. I've asked this before, but were you so afraid of success that you self-destructed? Did you not feel worthy of the responsibility, or were you just a drunk? Were you lazy? Or did the depression you suffered from not allow you to get out of bed in the morning? Is it possible that society had diagnosed a very capable man as being lazy when he honestly could not drag himself out of bed to face the gray world? Jesus, Dad, if only you had been born thirty years later, maybe someone would have figured you out. Maybe this is why I'm writing about this now. Maybe this whole thing is a response to what you experienced so many years ago. It is possible that you're reaching out to others, through me, so they don't have to accept the same torment, injustice, abuse and reckoning that you did.

I hope that's what it is, Dad. I really do. I am sorry for what you went through. For what you put us through. For what you put my mother through. This book was not meant to put you down. It was only meant to shed light on both sides of this crazy, complicated equation. Hope I've made you proud, Dad.

LEGACY

What is yours, Dad? What did you want it to be? Is there a difference between what it is and what you hoped? I ask this because currently your legacy is not what most of us would consider . . . great. Sure, some may remember that you were tough, physically; but in this day and age, that does not carry the same currency that it did in the 1970s. Are we, the survivors of your reign of terror, your legacy? If we are, well then, I have to admit that you should be proud. Of course, on the surface, it appears that you had nothing to do with our individual successes; however, perhaps despite you, each one of your children have succeeded. And make no mistake, we have *all* succeeded. There is not a person alive who could have predicted just how successful each of us has become. We were dirty, poor, trailer park trash. Yet not one of us has followed in your footsteps. We all provide for our families, we all have careers—in fact, one of your daughters has a university degree. I'm so proud of her. She accomplished this while caring for her son on her own. That's a legacy. She sacrificed her personal and professional life to raise a child while she went to school and got her degree.

What did you sacrifice, Dad? What did you do to make any one of us better? Did you ever, for one moment, think about putting the bottle down for the betterment of your children? Wait, I know the answer to that question. You did not. Never in the short period of time I knew you did you ever put our well-being before your own. You looked after yourself first, and then, if there were any scraps left . . . you threw them to us. Do you have any idea how that makes a child feel? Do you have any idea how that makes an adult feel when they look back on their life and reflect on their relationship with their father? I hope not. No, I know that you do not—you did not. You cared only about yourself. Had you been an accountant, me, my brother and sisters would have appeared in the debit column. We were an expense. A liability. I often wonder if you ever thought it would have been easier to kill us all instead of killing yourself . . . But it's pretty difficult to dispose of five bodies, so I guess maybe this never crossed your mind. Well, maybe never crossed your mind . . . practically.

In some strange way, is the survival of your children and wife your legacy? That you chose to not take us with you on your final journey the one mark you left on society? You allowed us to continue on with our lives as you ended yours.

But I really don't think that you put that much thought into it, as much as I'd like to think you did.

No, maybe at one point in time you gave us the luxury of living by firing bullets over our heads instead of into them, but I still do not believe that you thought far enough into the future to imagine just how we could all survive without you. Did you think our world would end when you ended yours?

It did not. We still live on after you pulled that trigger and the echo of that rifle blast is still being heard forty years later by each one of us.

THE DREAM HOUSE

I don't know if there is any one definition of a "dream house." For me, the phrase has many meanings. Dad, what did it mean to you? I remember, as we drove out to that farmhouse in Horton Township, that your brother, who followed in his car with his family, said he'd give his right arm to live in a place like that. Well, we had just moved from a tent trailer parked in an abandoned church parking lot. And, in retrospect, I cannot imagine where he and his family were living . . .

So, did your dream house have a fence? Was there a level, green lawn? Did you have visions of a dog running around trying to find a place to bury a bone? Or was your version more of what we had far too often, a place that was remote with no telephone? A place where you could keep us hostage? A place where, because my mother did not drive, you knew you would always find us? A place where you could control and contain us? There was no joy in any of the places you put us, with maybe the exception of the house in Elliot Lake. Of course, in Elliot Lake you were sober, and we were almost equals amongst our peers. Almost—not quite. We were always "the dirty LaPorte kids." I'm not sure why, but we were. That "dream house" did nothing to scrub away the ever-present grime.

I've had a few dream houses, Dad, and you had nothing to do with any of them. I bought them, for the most part on my own, through hard work, blood, sweat and tears, and some help from Suzie's parents. Sure, we had to pay them back, but they allowed us to get into our first dream house.

Fast-forward a few profitable years in business and a few bad business decisions later, and we had moved into and out of what was probably in most people's minds a true "dream house." The place was 150 years old and completely renovated. We had added a pool and a detached garage that most men would envy.

The question is, Dad, was this truly a dream house? I ask this because it honestly broke my heart to move out of the place. Suzie and I had scrimped and saved to be able to afford to live in a house like this, but at the end of the day we weren't happy there. And I will honestly accept responsibility for that. She did nothing wrong. But I, as the land baron that I was, spent too much time with my friends enjoying the fruits of my labours and, in the process, not only lost my land, but almost lost my wife. Honestly, she just wanted to spend time with me, but I was too busy spending time with my buddies to fully appreciate her. Jesus, she put up with a lot. She still does, but nowhere near what I put her through over at the dream house.

Did you ever come close to that realization, Dad— where you finally understood that your relationship with my mother was more important than your relationship with your buddies? I know the answer. And to be honest, it took me almost thirty years of marriage to come to the realization myself. I know that my friendships are important, but the older I get, the more I appreciate Suzie. It's crazy, right? Maybe if you had hung in there a little longer you might have realized that whoever you were having a relationship with at the time was more important than you and your buddies. Maybe you would have realized, like me, that your dream house did not have to be a perfect house, but rather an imperfect home.

THE NIGHTMARE

I had another dream the other night, and it disturbed me so much that I woke up and could not fall back asleep. I immediately texted both kids to see if they were okay because both were out. It was around one thirty on a Saturday morning.

Did I dream that one of them was in an accident? No.

Did I think someone had hurt one of them? Yes.

Who had caused the pain?

I did.

The dream was about Eric and me. We were in a dark hallway in some building I've never been in before. The walls were gray and dirty, and the sconces on them projected barely enough light for me to recognize my own boy.

We were facing each other, only inches apart. He and I were having some sort of argument that my dream state did not allow me to fully understand or appreciate. He poked me in my chest with two fingers while he was making a point. I told him not to poke me and got very defensive. Then he got defensive too.

Before I knew it, we were wrapped up in each other's arms in a struggle for control. I did what I always did with a bigger and stronger opponent, I grabbed him, took out his legs and drove him to the ground, directing him head-first. His skull struck the floor with a thud and even in my dream state I was horrified. I had completely lost control and forgot that this was my son and not some criminal I was trying to apprehend and did the only thing that I was capable of doing. I incapacitated my opponent. I've done this successfully many times while making an arrest, but, Jesus, this was my son . . . I love this boy more than I love life itself. What animalistic instinct took over that would ever allow me to do that to him, even subconsciously?

I did not wake up, even though I wanted to.

In my nightmare, we lay on the floor, me waiting to see the damage I'd done to this beautiful boy. He struggled to get to his feet. I was on my knees looking up at him and was afraid of what I'd see. Did I smash his face beyond repair? I didn't know. I honestly didn't. It was awful while I waited for him to stand and turn his face to me.

When he did, the result was even worse than I had anticipated. His face was not damaged or broken. It was intact, but his expression was sad. So very, very sad.

He never spoke a word, he just turned and looked at me. His big brown, sad eyes, staring at me, questioning me, until a single tear rolled out of one of his eyes. In that moment

I could not understand if he was hurt because of what I had done to him physically or mentally. I think I know the answer, and it pains me more than anything I could ever imagine. This was the worst nightmare I've ever had, and I have no explanation for it.

I love my son. He is such a good boy. In my waking hours, even though he has made me angry in the past, I've never felt so angry that I would ever harm him. Never. This is my boy. I am so proud of him, and I wish I knew why the hell this type of dream could enter into my subconscious.

But this does bring me back to you, Dad, and your relationship with your father and the physical fights that I know you had.

Did you ever feel badly after you put him in the hospital?

What could he have possibly said that would put you in such a rage that you were compelled to strike him?

I am horrified about what happened between me and my son *in a dream*. Were you horrified the day you and I want back to your father's house after one of your battles? There was a lot of blood. Was it his, or was it yours? I suspect it was his—he was the one in the hospital, after all. Was it something he said to you, or was it something you said to him? Maybe it was something he did to you when you were younger, and you were finally getting your revenge? Were you finally becoming the man of the house? Is that why you brought me with you when you went to clean up and grab some of his personal items to take to the hospital? Did you want to show me what would happen if I stepped out of line as an adult, or did you want to give me a glimpse into our future? Is this what you saw for us? Was it expected that I would grab some clothes for you and take them to the hospital after one of our bouts? Or maybe you were trying to reinforce just how tough you were so that I never tried to challenge you the way you challenged your father. Maybe you were trying to teach me a lesson. Maybe you wanted me to see the aftermath of a father-son brawl. Well, Dad, you don't need to worry about that. I've never struck my son and never will. That nightmare is the closest I'll ever come; and even though it wasn't real, it's a memory that will haunt me forever.

THE COSMIC COLLISION

You know, Dad, I've really tried to keep from exposing the real me to the people I work with. It's not that I've acted like someone I'm not, it's just that I've kept hidden the part of me that I'm embarrassed or, frankly, afraid of. I try so very hard to keep the damaged Brent away from those who either work with me or for me. I avoid judgment. I don't want pity. I want people to see me as I am today. Honest, productive, empowering—a leader. I have been the lowest of the low, and I have experienced success as an executive. There are very few I talk to about either my successes or my failures. I try very hard to lead by example. I work hard. I make business decisions every day and try to evaluate the human currency in relation to the business currency. As Marc, my boss, has often said: I have a very high empathy score. It's a difficult thing to balance managing people *and* the bottom line. Still, I honestly believe I am doing a good job at it. The people who report to me are my most valuable asset. I want to empower them. I want them to want to come to work every day. Am I successful at this a hundred percent of the time? Clearly not, or I would not be writing about the "Cosmic Collision," would I, Dad?

Unfortunately, I had to let an employee go a few weeks ago. It did not go well. The details are unimportant, other than this: the employee refused to leave the building and at one point shoved me. I stood firm, and it took every ounce of restraint not to hit him. He then shoved me a second time . . .

The next thing I recall is him lying on the floor and people gathering around. I felt awful—not because I defended myself, but because I had exposed this side of me to my colleagues. I have spent my entire adult life trying to keep this Brent from those who work with and for me. Make no mistake, I don't regret my actions. The guy got what he deserved. (In all honesty, less than he deserved—I later learned he was reaching for a hidden knife.) And if he wasn't an employee, and I hadn't been trying my best to protect our company, I may have not stopped by just putting him on his ass. I contained the rage that was running through my veins as he confronted me. I let him know that fifty-one-year-old Brent was not afraid of twenty-something him. He hurled insults and threats, not fully understanding the rage that was boiling under my skin. As an executive of the company, I would never expose either the company or myself to any legal jeopardy . . . Yet for days and weeks after the incident, which was captured on video, my co-workers offered me congratulations for how

I handled this situation. I'm embarrassed, Dad. I don't want to be congratulated for knocking this guy on his ass. I don't want to be remembered for being able to take down an aggressor. I want to leave that part of me behind. I am trying so hard to erase the LaPorte Curse. I'm not trying to be the toughest man in town like you. I want to be known for more than that. But for Christ's sake, Dad, it seems like I cannot escape the pattern of violence. I didn't want this, Dad. I spent at least ten minutes trying to talk this guy out of the office, yet for some goddamn reason he wanted to fight. What is it about us that makes violence a part of who we are? Do we have personalities or faces that people just want to hate, or is it just the stars we were born under, where no matter how much we grow and change as adults that we cannot escape the inevitable? Am I a child born of violence who will lead a life of violence whether or not I am looking for it? How the hell is this fair? I'm doing my best to be peaceable, and every once in a while I'm asked by the universe to step up and do the right thing . . . It just isn't fair. Why won't someone else step up for once? I'm tired, Dad. Really tired. I just want . . . to be.

Is this how you felt at the end? Maybe you were tired of fighting all your buddies' battles. Maybe you were tired of fighting your own. Maybe the only way you could see to stop the fighting was to stop fighting yourself and to end it all. Is it possible, Dad, that you saw no end to the conflict, and the only way to get some peace was to shut off?

If there's no Barry LaPorte, then there's no more conflict.

I kind of get it. Your solution was to check out of the fight and let everyone else sort it out. I still disagree with your decision, but I may be closer to understanding it than I've ever been. And while it may have brought peace to you, it brought hell to the rest of us. I do wish you would have fought for life the way you fought so many men over the years. I wish you would not have submitted to the impulse to give up. I wish you would have fought as fiercely against *all* your impulses. Maybe things would have been different. Then again, maybe they would have been worse.

DAMAGED BUT NOT BROKEN

I think that most of us are damaged, but are we really broken? My "glass half full" perspective is that we are not. Everyone on the planet—even those we consider the most successful— has had some bumps and bruises. That doesn't mean that when the chips are down we simply fold like a cheap suit . . . No, it means that we should recognize, evaluate and take control of our lives. Control the situation, or it will control you. An alien race might describe humanity as a basket of bruised apples. Sure, you may not want to take a bite out of one, but collectively we could make one hell of a pie. Cut off the bruises, and we are pretty damn good. Add a little brown sugar, butter, cinnamon . . .

I try to remind myself, Dad, that while I may not be perfect, I'm pretty damn good. And that is not so bad.

SAFE PLACE

I think in every house I've ever owned I created a "safe" or "happy" place. I think most people do the same thing. Maybe it's a man cave, sewing room, kitchen, garage or cozy living room. I believe it's in our nature to create some sort of space where we can be comfortable, where we relax and forget about the day's problems.

For me it's always been the garage. I remember the garage in the first home I owned. It was a small and narrow garage with barely enough room for a vehicle. The previous owner had left a few older tools, a yardstick and some other odds and ends. I kept them around me to remind me of the history of the home and to give me comfort. I would spend hours out in that cold shop in the winter, building things, working on my car or just tooling around. I expect most men are like this. I am not sure why we are this way, but it is a fact, most of us like to be surrounded by tools and gadgets.

Did you ever have a place like this, Dad? And where was it? Sadly, it was probably a bar or hotel. Would things have been different if you'd had a place you could go to tinker around with things that needed painting or fixing? I know that more often than not we barely had a house to live in, and when you throw in five kids and a wife, maybe asking for a happy place would be too much. Or is it? I'm a strong believer in finding your "happy place" so that when times are tough, or frankly, when they are not, you have a place to go and just sit. Not to talk or watch TV necessarily, but to just be.

Just be. That is one of the things I remind myself, and I do believe that my time alone, enjoying my surroundings and not thinking about anything has helped keep me somewhat sane.

Just be.

Think about it. Dad, if you had the ability to "just be," maybe you wouldn't have pulled the trigger. Maybe you would have been satisfied with what you had around you and had the wisdom to be grateful for the people in your world.

My current garage is my safe place. I have surrounded myself with items that make me happy and grateful for my family and friends. I have arts and crafts that my kids gave me on my wall; ticket stubs from sporting events and movies that my kids and I attended are present, as are a couple of items from my family's past. A bucket of old horseshoes sits in the corner of my shop, as does an old bucksaw my grandpa Frankie used when he worked in the bush as a young man. I look at that rusted old saw, put my hands on the one surviving handle and get great comfort knowing that he too, once held the same piece of wood that I am holding.

Speaking of Grandpa Frankie, I would be remiss not to mention that if he didn't start the "just be" state of mind, he perfected it. I also have to state that his house was my first real home. My first real safe place. My first happy place. This is a testament to him and Grandma Molly who always made me feel welcome and safe. I miss them both dearly.

They lived in an old blacksmith shop on the shores of the Calabogie Lake; he converted it into a home when he returned to Canada after WWII with my Grandma Molly in tow from Scotland. I spent almost every summer of my childhood and all of my teen years at that poorly insulated, cold, drafty old house. I was never warmer in my life.

Proof positive that the structure does not make a house a home. It is the people inside that have the ability to transform it.

The house was built on a pretty good chunk of the Canadian Shield, so the backyard was a rocky hill. My grandpa Frankie tried and succeeded in turning the top into a small garden. How he kept it going, I have no idea because there was no running water—and no irrigation. Still, he grew a small garden and sat for hours and hours at the top of that hill at a picnic table, watching the green onions grow. He never took a book to read. He sometimes took a portable radio, and more often than not a beer. That man could sit and "cypher" as he called it. For hours and hours, he could just be.

We did not disturb him when he was in his happy place. The thoughts that were running through his fertile mind, well, I can only imagine. Or maybe not. He was a smart man. He would often test me with riddles to see if I could come up with the solution. I believe this is where I got my love for problem-solving.

This was his place to just be.

To the chagrin of my wife and kids, I've inherited that quality. I can sit for long periods, and simply think quietly. About what? Again, who knows.

I cannot write about this happy place without explaining my relationship with my Grandma Molly. She was one of a kind and my best friend. The last time I cried at a funeral was for Grandpa Frankie. While I was obviously sad at his passing, I was absolutely devastated when, at the funeral, I had received Communion and while walking back to my seat, noticed my Grandma Molly weeping at her pew over the loss of her husband. She was inconsolable. I could not stand to see this amazing woman in such pain, and there was nothing I could do to ease it. I was now inconsolable. I didn't cry for me, Dad; I cried for her. I don't think I've cried that hard at any other time in my life.

I felt more connected to that woman than almost anyone else on earth. She was tough. She had a great sense of humour. When she laughed, it made you want to laugh. When she was mad, it made you afraid. She was not a morning person, so you did not talk to her before she'd had her tea and was fully awake.

I spent countless hours sitting at her kitchen table drinking tea when I should have been doing homework. I'd take the B or C on a test just to sit with her. I wouldn't change a single thing.

She had the wisdom to understand who she was and where she was—living in a house with no plumbing—and appreciate it. I never heard her complain.

I think it is important for all of us to understand and respect when our spouses or children need that alone time to sit and do nothing. I think it is healthy. Not being productive can be good for the soul. It is something I will try to remember the next time I want to chastise one of my kids for doing nothing.

I've felt so strongly about this Just Be idea that I tried to help a friend of mine create a web-based business around it. (Unfortunately, there was another website with the same idea.) This did not stop me from having and enjoying my own safe place where I could Just Be.

There is something to be said for creating an environment full of happy memories, celebrating them, and per Max Ehrmann ". . . in the noisy confusion of life, keep peace in your soul. With all its sham, drudgery and broken dreams, it is still a beautiful world. Be cheerful. Strive to be happy."

I wish you would have had a place to do this, Dad, I really do. You were a tortured man. We all know that. Would a safe, happy place have helped? I don't know. It certainly couldn't have hurt.

CLIMBING TREES

Have you ever climbed a tree, Dad? I have. There's one tree
I'm thinking about specifically. You and Mom had been sep-
arated for a while, and we were living in a small wartime
house in Renfrew. There was a large maple tree in the centre
of the backyard. I can't tell you how many times I climbed it
just to sit, look over the world and think. There was something peaceful about being high above everyone else in the
neighbourhood. I am not sure why we climb trees—maybe it
has something to do with our primal instincts. Is it because
when the apes are in danger they climb their way to safety;
is that why?

During that period of my life, when I was upset or angry,
more often than not I found myself climbing higher and
higher, seeking the embrace of that old maple's branches.

The foliage would protect me from the judging eyes of other kids. When I was in that tree, I was above everyone else. Hidden both physically and emotionally. The tree was my silent protector. My confidante. My friend.

Crazy to say that a tree could be a trusted friend, but it was. It was a living and productive resident of this earth, so why not? I've sat and cried in that tree more than I care to admit. When you died, and when I realized just how poor, dirty and despondent I was. This was my life as a nine-year-old. The tree was there when no one else was. It never judged me or my status. Life seemed so hard back then, but also, as I look at it in the rear-view mirror, so simple.

When Suzie and I took possession of our dream house, there were many beautiful maple trees on the property, and the first thing I did, the day we got the keys, was drive my truck around back with a cooler full of ice-cold beer. I sat under an awesome hundred-foot-tall tree and completely relaxed for the first time in years. I felt so comfortable and safe watching its outstretched limbs sway in the summer breeze as I listened to the music created by the rustling leaves and creaking limbs. This symphony was conducted just for me.

Have you ever had that feeling, Dad? Was there anything that you did that made you so relaxed and safe, where you felt that nothing or no one in the world could possibly harm you? Maybe it wasn't climbing a tree. Maybe it was climbing under the hood of a '69 Chevelle. Was that your happy place? Did a finely tuned carburetor have the same effect on you that creaking limbs had on me? Was the smell of vinyl seats as comforting to you as fresh-cut grass was to me? Or maybe you were comforted by the lake? The same lake that I look out on as I write this.

There was one day you, Barrie and I were out, and you picked up a pizza and drove us to sit by Calabogie Lake as we ate. You seemed so relaxed and happy that maybe, just maybe this was your happy place. Your maple tree. I have never known you to go out on the lake, in fact I cannot recall ever even seeing you in or on the water. Could you swim?

Did you find peace in the sound of the waves crashing on the shore? I know I have. I love this lake. It's mine—it really is. I spent my high school years carrying water from it when I lived with Grandpa Frankie and Grandma Molly, because they had no running water. I drank from it, bathed in it, swam in it, played in it and sat beside it on countless nights, just staring at the stars and the moon and reflecting while my buddies were out at a bar. Like my maple tree, this lake was cleansing to my body and my soul. Did you feel the same way? With every wave that came in and out, I felt reborn. I was baptized by the beauty and purity. The blue waters, sparkling with untouchable diamonds, was and still is a great source of peace for me. My friends don't understand it. Suzie doesn't fully understand it, and maybe I really don't understand it either. But when I'm driving home, turning that last curve on the highway that brings me to a small hill where I can finally see the lake, *my lake*, I begin to unwind.

I guess the difference between you and me is that I have the ability to recognize a safe and happy place. Maybe you never had that. Maybe your mind wouldn't allow you to get there. Maybe you wouldn't allow yourself to get there. It's not easy, I can tell you that. In order to find and accept a state of mind, you have to surrender yourself to the place and time. Is it possible that an inability to surrender was what kept you from ever being truly happy? Is it this loss of control that scared you and prevented you from just being?

Did serenity scare you? Did chaos always rule the day? Did you seek your energy from drama and confrontation rather than from the natural forces of the world around you? I have people in my life who live for drama, never recognizing the beauty of the things around them. These people tend to eat other people's energy. Draining their very lifeblood, like a vampire. I try to avoid these people because after we interact I am exhausted. I still really do look at things like a child, simply and with hope for better things to come.

I suppose this is why at fifty-one I can still feel the comfort, warmth and affection of something inanimate like a tree or a lake. I guess this is why I would be looked at by some as "simple." Show me a shiny object, and I'll stare. I accept that, because I'd rather be the guy who gets taken advantage of than the guy who is taking advantage of others. I try not to be suspicious until someone gives me a reason to be suspicious. I do not start relationships with suspicion on my mind. Maybe that's why I'm not a great businessman, and why I suppose I never will be. Again, I'll take that trade all day long, because I look for the best in others. If a person treats me wrong, that is on them, not me. Yes, maybe I'm gullible—I can be tricked. You knew this, Dad, when you told me you were going out that night to help the police. The difference is that I sleep pretty well at night. (Despite the nightmares.)

For the record, my conscience is not one hundred percent clear. I've done many things I regret. But when I did these things, I never intentionally set out to hurt anyone. Those I've harmed in the past, I have not forgotten. I just have to reconcile with the fact that I cannot turn back time and change what I've done. In order for me to go on, I have to sit by my lake or under a tree, reflect and pray that I will be a better man tomorrow.

THE VILLAGE

I think of Hillary Clinton writing about how "it takes a village," Dad.

She was not wrong, you know.

A village can help change a man, for better or for worse. I know this, Dad, and you knew this too. We each have a village, or town, or city that has affected us beyond what any of us can comprehend. For me, Calabogie was a positive influence. For you, Renfrew was clearly negative. I suppose that's why I have had such an issue with that town—because of what it did to you.

As I've said, I spent a lot of time in this small Ottawa Valley village, mostly with my grandparents, but also during the first five years of my life. I started school there, made my first friends there, learned to swim there and fell in love for the first time there. It's also where I had my heart broken and where I learned to drink and fight. I played more hockey on that beaten-down outdoor rink than I did just about anywhere else in the world.

I was reminded this past week when I was back home visiting with my friends, reminiscing about our high school years. I finally had the opportunity to say to them, openly and honestly, that they and the people in this village rescued me. As men, we rarely openly share this type of emotional news, but it was important to me to let them know that this is a fact. You see, Dad, after you tore us from the arms of the community in Calabogie and dragged our entire family halfway across Ontario, I'd finally returned to my roots. My village: my people. Sure, I was different, because of what I'd experienced, but not that different that the lads did not accept me back into the fold.

Each and every one of these men (kids at the time) allowed me to come to their town during the summer months as I tried to escape our reputation in Renfrew. Okay, it really wasn't the town of Renfrew I had a problem with—it was and is all of the horrible memories, the places and the people who did nothing to stop the horror show that was playing in every house we lived in. I don't mean to sound like a broken record, but that's how I felt. How I feel. Misplaced anger, maybe, but an open and honest reaction to a very troubling time.

The real beauty of these Calabogie guys is that even though I had to fight my way into the group, some sort of initiation I'm sure, they did welcome me. When I came to town on weekends, they included me; when I was there for the summer with my grandparents, I was allowed to play ball for the Calabogie Eagles. Now I'm sure some of the lads knew our history, but they never mentioned it. Mainly because many of them had their own history with their own fathers or mothers. We all carried some sort of battle scar and, honestly, until adulthood, never spoke of them. We played together and eventually worked together. We drank together and loved together. And, yes, we fought. But we always, always understood each other, and somehow the dial returned to zero and balance in our friendships returned. I am proud of the group of men that we have become. Each of us has some damn issue and have all overcome it to become active, productive members of society. It really is amazing when I sit back and think about it.

But Dad, you were not so fortunate in your "village," were you? Your group included many followers and lackies. Each one standing beside you at the bar, egging you on to one more fight. Each wanted to be the guy next to the guy who just wiped the floor with some other guy. They never pulled you out of a bar as I've done with my buddies, and they've done with me. While your pals may have said they had your back, they in reality did not. Mine did. As you cruised the bars in Renfrew, looking for excitement at the urging of your buddies, did you ever stop to question their motives? Did any one of them ever tell you to save your money and go home to your wife and five kids? I'm guessing not. And what would you have said to them if they had? Maybe he would have been the guy getting picked up off of the bar floor.

I'd like to ask you, Dad, what hold did Renfrew have on you? But I know the answer—because Calabogie has the same hold on me. When I drive along the shoreline of that lake and hear the water rushing over the dam, I know I'm home. Suzie does not always understand, but this is where

I found true friends. Where, for the first time in my life, I felt accepted. I felt a part of a group that had the same issues I did. Even though we never spoke of them, we just knew. I grew into a man there. I made so many mistakes in this dot on the map, but for the most part, the people, the fabric of this community always forgave me. Always gave me another shot at redemption. They did not condone my behaviour, for sure, but despite the glances I may have received at the store or in church the next day, they always welcomed me back with open arms.

I expect this was the same with you and Renfrew. You always had a buddy to welcome you back and hand you that "first" beer. The difference is that my community accepted me for who I really was. Or, maybe your community accepted you for who you really were as well, and that's why you were always drawn back. If that's the case I'd have to believe that the real you was a monster and that they knew and liked that. I'm not sure who this reflects more poorly on . . . you or them. One guy going off the rails; his so-called friends controlling the switches to ensure that he jumped the tracks.

ALCOHOL

I'm actually going to cut you a bit of slack here, Dad, because alcohol abuse has plagued me too. It's often the same question: "Why do you drink so much?" Not great for me to be admitting that I've been asked this question, but I have. The truth is: I like beer. I like the taste of it and how it makes me feel. I've had to reassure Suzie that when I'm having a bad day because of work or life, or if I'm just feeling blue, that I am more apt to sneak through a drive-through and grab a Big Mac rather than reach for a beer. I think it's important to note that food offers as much comfort to some of us as alcohol or drugs do to others. Both have health implications that should be addressed—just not here. While I'm not saying that I've not used alcohol as a way to numb some of my pain, it is simply not my first choice when I'm feeling down. It has always been and will likely always be food. I continue to work on this part of my life. Me driving by a fast-food restaurant is much like an alcoholic driving by a bar.

Instead of asking people why they drink too much or eat too much, why don't we ask, "What's wrong?" Maybe it's the same question—but I don't think so.

Dad, did anyone ever ask you what was wrong? How would you have answered? I mean, if someone you truly respected and cared about sat you down in a serious manner and asked you if you were okay . . . how would that have gone? Would you have brushed it off and said nothing, as most of us do? Would you have been angry at the notion that the great Barry LaPorte could have an emotional problem? Do you think you would have been seen as less of a man if you admitted to having some sort of issue? Do you think that if you admitted to this that maybe, just maybe, it might have helped?

I wonder if we can begin to rephrase the question and not look at the alcohol or drug abuse as the problem but ask the user what the problem is. Would that make a difference? I'm sure counselling professionals do this every day, as they ask their clients *why*. But my question is why does the question always includes the drinking, drugs or food? It only puts me on the defensive, as though how I'm choosing to deal with my issues is now also on trial. So now I have to account for my poor coping mechanism *and* my issues. I mean, what do you want to talk about, my eating being out of control or the reason behind it? Now I not only have to open up about past abuse or bad experiences, but I also have to feel like a pig because I eat too much as a way to satiate a part of my brain that is gratified by this poor choice.

I'm not talking about therapists here. I'm talking about our friends, family, co-workers who, for no fault of their own, phrase these questions this way. I think if we can all take a step back and just ask our friends in need what is wrong and what we can do to help—without putting their entire life on trial—that maybe we can be a little more helpful. Maybe if we make those who need help feel a little less judged they might open up to us as to what the real issue is.

Do you think this may have helped you, Dad? Do you think that if those around you had asked why you were so angry, so sad, so volatile that things could have ended differently? Did you ever open up to anyone about what happened in your past that made you feel the way you did? Do you think that if you did open up that anyone would have understood? Did they have the capacity to process and empathize with what you had been through? Were they willing to understand, if they could even comprehend what you were trying to tell them? I suspect they had none of these qualities. I've met them, and honestly, I seriously doubt their capacity for empathy. Nice group of friends you had there.

Thankfully, my village is full of empathetic people with the capacity to understand that forgiveness is not a free pass to future bad behaviour. They hold me accountable—and that's a blessing.

CUTTING GRASS

You know, Dad, in the few years we were together, I can't remember you ever cutting the grass. That's not to say that you didn't. Someone obviously did; I don't remember our lawn being overgrown. But when did you find the time? And when you did—if you did—did you find the same peace in doing it that I do? You know, I'm fifty-one, and I get the same feeling today that I had when I was twenty-three and mowing the lawn of my first house.

Many people curse this chore. Not me, I relish in it. I feel so fortunate that I actually have a lawn that I swore a long time ago to never be upset at having to cut it. I clearly remember when Suzie and I purchased our first home. We lived on a hill and the lawn mower was always in danger of tipping over because of the grade. I think there may have been one time early on when I was frustrated about it but then grabbed myself by the collar—as I often try to do—and told myself, "You are lucky to be able to afford a house with a lawn to cut." The message got through. I felt and still feel truly blessed to have this chore. There are so many people in so many countries who pray for rain so that they can turn a patch of dirt into something green.

What did you think of when you cut the grass, Dad? Work? Our family situation? Or about where you were going that night? The men you'd go drinking with at the bar, or the women you'd meet?

Cutting grass is maybe the greatest form of therapy I know. For the most part, it's mindless. Just make sure you have gas and oil in the mower, start it . . . and away you go.

I've been cutting grass since I was ten. I used to drag an old lawn mower around our neighbourhood, knocking on doors to make five bucks a lawn. I did this for years, and after I turned twelve, my mother no longer had to buy my clothes. Mowing grass was not only my source of income but also my source of solitude. I've solved countless world and personal problems while pushing or pulling a Tecumseh engine around lawns. As I reflect, it really is mind boggling. Fight with the girlfriend—cut a lawn. School trouble—cut a lawn. Going to college—cut a lawn. Honestly, many of my major life decisions were made standing behind a hunk of steel with a motor that churned a blade at who knows how many revolutions per minute.

It continued when I spent summers with my grand-parents, as my grandfather was the custodian of a school in that small village. My brother and I would cut the grass while he worked inside, polishing floors. My brother was much better at cutting the grass than I was—but I pushed that lawn mower around what at the time seemed like several football fields every summer, all summer, until Grandpa Frankie retired.

After that I started cutting grass for all of their friends who were either too old or didn't want to cut their own grass. The money I made helped me pay for the things that Mom couldn't afford. More importantly, I've had more real conversations with myself pushing a lawn mower in concentric rectangles than most people have with their spouses during a thirty-year marriage. Doing this as a teen I always had my Walkman on—also paid for with grass-cutting money. I listened to the same teen angst–influenced music that millions of other teens were listening to.

I loved it, Dad. I really did.

I guess I was fortunate that I had a grandpa who would allow a ten-year-old boy to take two weeks to cut a school lawn when it should have taken two days. I know now that it must have been painful for him to silently watch me pull that lawn mower out of its hiding place at the back of the Catholic nuns' residence and drag it to the back field where for the next two weeks I would butcher his grass. He was a good man, Dad. I expect you knew that. It didn't change how you treated his daughter, but you must have seen how he dealt with things. How he would let a person make a mistake and then quietly clean it up afterwards so as to not embarrass them.

Did you have anyone like this in your life, Dad? I know you were handy. You could fix just about anything that was put in front of you. Who taught you? Certainly not your dad, because the only thing Rudy was capable of fixing was a drink. Seriously, as I write this and think of the people who have influenced and mentored me, I'm forced to acknowledge that there must have been someone who took you under their wing. There must have been someone who, at some point, handed you a wrench and had the confidence in you to allow you to either tighten or loosen a bolt. Was it a teacher at RCI? Maybe you got a job as an apprentice at a garage at a young age and showed an aptitude? There must have been one man in your life who saw something in you that no one else saw. I'd like to talk to that guy. I'd like to know if when he saw your potential he also saw the flaws in your character. Did he ever speak to you about them, Dad? Did you spend countless hours with this man, following him around his garage, learning all you could about how things work . . . and then maybe one day, he spoke to you about how you treated my mom or another woman, and you shut him down? Did Rudy intercede, seeing how much time you were spending with your mentor, and plant seeds of doubt in your mind about your mentor's true motive? Rudy was sly like that, but we both know that. Is it possible, Dad, that there is, or was, a man out there that knows more about the true you than anyone else on the planet? Logic tells me that there was one person who helped you become the mechanic you became. Maybe I'm creating a story where there isn't one: creating a character who tried to keep you on the straight and narrow as the rebel in you rebuked him in a final act of independence. Maybe I'm creating a romantic version of events that never occurred. That's my prerogative, right? Because you're not here to answer my questions. That is also my problem, I suppose: I'm a romantic by nature. As a storyteller, I create both sides of a tale, and I often, in turn, create a history that is not always plausible.

So what does it all have to do with cutting grass? A lot. Grandpa Frankie did not really show me how to cut grass, but he also never told me how not to cut grass. He let me figure this out for myself. I still, to this day, take so much pride in how I cut my grass. It's not a neighbourhood pride thing, it's a Brent thing. If it is not cut to my standards, I will cut it again. I think anyone thinking this way can replace cutting grass with sewing a dress, making a bed, washing a dish, cleaning a wrench, welding metal, editing a book or performing complicated engineering calculations. We all just want it done right. We can't help ourselves. Call it perfectionism. That might be what it is. But maybe not. Maybe we just want things done the way we want them done. Who knows what took place in our past that forces us to do things a certain way? Is it wrong to want to do things the way we want them done? I don't think so. It really only causes an issue when we push these expectations on others who maybe don't see it the same way we do. Thankfully, Grandpa Frankie never did this. He just let me find my way. He let me discover my own mistakes, and as I grew and could see what I'd done, correct the flaws and learn how not to make the same mistakes again. This is wisdom, Dad. But I'm pretty sure that while I experienced Grandpa's process, I've not always followed it. Frankie had a gentle way of teaching that took time and patience. I'm not sure I have enough of either of those things.

HOCKEY

Seems strange to ask you about hockey. Or maybe not. Maybe hockey is the most logical thing for a Canadian kid to ask his father about. If we were in the States, I'd be asking about baseball or football; anywhere else in the world, I'm sure it would be soccer. But here I am with questions about your feelings toward the sport. Not just the sport, but everything around it. The things that make us so passionate about hockey.

Some of the best and worst times I've had with my kids have involved this crazy, brutal, beautiful game. I taught both kids to skate by the time they were three. Tried to get them both to play. While Angèle did not play, she knows more about hockey than most grown men. She will sit on the couch with me and yell at the Habs as much as or more than I do.

Eric played high-level hockey his entire life. I've spent countless hours at the rink coaching him and watching him practise and play. He is still my favourite player to watch. He has skill, speed and toughness that most players just do not have.

I played too, Dad. Did you know that?

I cannot clearly remember when I fell in love with hockey but do know it was around the time I fell in love with the Montreal Canadiens.

It was the mid '70s and they were winning everything. We were Habs fans. With a last name like LaPorte, we had to be.

Again, some of my fondest memories of you were when you were sober up in Elliot Lake and we'd watch hockey on a Saturday night. The TV was one of those big wooden console sets with a record player on one end. We'd lie in front of the TV with our elbows propped up on pillows and watch hockey together until it was time for you to go play.

I remember how I'd go down into the basement and climb into your hockey bag before you left for your game and crawl around your hockey gear, hold your shin pads up to me, imagine I was going to play with you. Your shin pads came up to my shoulders. Either I was very small, or you were very tall. After you'd left for the local rink, I'd run back to the TV hoping to catch a glimpse of you playing. I had no concept that those players were hundreds if not thousands of miles away from me and you.

You never took us to watch you play. Up until now I never really thought of that.

I've played organized hockey since I was twelve. You were dead for two or three years by then. Other than introducing me to the game, you had nothing to do with my hockey experiences. There is a man in Renfrew who did, however; his name is Brian Riley. He is dead now, but I'll never forget him. Once again, another man stepped up where you should have. This man paid for my first two years of hockey and my stepfather, Donnie, took me to every six-a.m. game and practice. These men gave me a lifelong love of the sport. I played until a couple of years ago.

Brian and Donnie have my gratitude. They were great men whose legacy lives on in the kids who I was privileged enough to help, encourage and coach. Some of those kids played in the OHL, and one, hopefully, will be playing in the NHL very soon—all because of the kindness and love shown by two men to a boy who was not even their own.

With all its violence and brutality, hockey really is beautiful.

I've met some of the best friends I have because of hockey. Did you make any friends playing hockey, Dad? I can't imagine you didn't. In fact, up until Elliot Lake, I didn't know that you ever played. Not sure how I could have as I was only four or five years old, but you would think I may have picked up on it. What position did you play? Were you a scoring forward, a tough defenceman? Maybe you were just there as a tough guy. Should I fill this gap in our history with visions of you going toe to toe with the toughest player on the other team? You defending your goalie by grabbing the biggest guy on the other team by the jersey, flipping it over his head and filling him in? Or will I be better served remembering you skating and scoring like Guy Lafleur? While I would prefer the latter, I expect it's not the truth.

HEROES

Since I can remember, I've always wanted to save the world or at least those around me from harm. I'm certainly not a hero, but dammit I wanted to be one. Like Atticus Finch, I've always wanted to be on the side of right. It seems ridiculous that a four-year-old boy would sit and watch a black-and-white TV rooting for Perry Mason to not only catch but prosecute the bad guy, but there I was, entranced by his pursuit of justice. This was all part of my wanting to become a police officer—this incurable desire to protect and serve. I tried to stand up to bullies; I sat with the "odd" kids or social outcasts at school, in turn becoming one myself. I was likely already one, and maybe that was just the group I was destined to be with, relegated to. It doesn't matter. I still enjoy losing myself in Iron Man's or

Captain America's struggle to save not just Earth but the entire universe.

I guess I'm not that different than most men. Or women, for that matter. But if I am being honest, I actually don't think most women want to be superheroes. They just already are. I am fortunate to know a lot of incredible women who, every day, do amazing things for their families and friends. To me, Suzie and her group of friends have already achieved superhero status. I've witnessed the pain that comes from caring for your families and not one of you have wavered from your commitment. You all inspire me to be better every single day.

My question, Dad, is did you ever want to make a difference? Did you ever want to be a hero? Did you have a hero? Did you relate more to the superhero . . . or to the villain? It's an important question, because I believe that you probably related more to the bad guys. Was it because that was the easiest path? It's not easy to be a hero. People make fun of them. Look at Clark Kent and Peter Parker—they were happy to be nerds while guys like Billy the Kid and John Dillinger went out of their way to be seen as heroes by guys like you. Did you see yourself as Dillinger or Capone, fighting injustice in the justice system simply because those rules did not apply to you? Who did you most relate to, Al Capone or Eliot Ness? I'm pretty sure I know the answer, but I have to ask. I think we all have to ask ourselves this question. It should be part of every psychological exam. The answer is quite revealing. I guess at some point we all root for the Hollywood bad guy, but in all fairness, these are bad people, who have done bad things. Just like you, Dad. You did very bad things that have impacted the lives of your children and their children and possibly their children.

Quite a legacy. Really, it is.

Does good behaviour have the same impact? We are not often remembered for what we did right, just for what we did wrong. Why do so many people relate to those who have "sinned" rather than those who have not? Why is the Prodigal Son so revered when he finally returns? Are we actually celebrating his successful rehabilitation or his past transgressions? Everybody loves a repentant sinner. Not everybody loves a saint.

So is it better to be Capone and give the people what they want or to be Ness and follow the rule of law and do the "right" thing?

I always related to Ness. I expect, Dad, you related to Capone. Or Dillinger. Or William Boyd. You were the definition of a bad boy. You fought your way out of more bars than you walked out of peacefully.

I know you recognized the fact that I was more in the Ness camp from an early age. You had an ability to know what I was thinking as I was thinking it. You identified my early obsession with police officers and law and order and used it to disguise your own nefarious behaviour. There was that one early August evening when we were still living in the tent trailer by the highway. It was after supper, not yet dark but not completely light. The last of the day's gold fell across the adjacent farmer's fields, and you were once again leaving us for the night. I followed you to your hearse-black station wagon and asked where you were going. I watched you stuff a thick hose down the outside of one leg of your pants and was curious as to what this was for. You looked at me, smiled and told me you were going out to help the police. To this day, I have no idea what that hose was for, but at the time I believed you. I wanted to believe you. I was pretty gullible back then. I still am. Not a great trait, but I'm working on it.

Did I think you were a hero at the time? Possibly. Were you? Absolutely not.

YOUR GRAVE

Today I visited your grave for the first time in forty years. I wasn't even sure at first that I would find it. I was a child the last time I was in the cemetery, so I was not sure that I could even find your final resting place. But actually, I found it quickly—within minutes. There was an elderly groundskeeper cutting the grass, and he and I exchanged an awkward nod. While I had no clear recollection of where you were buried, I had literally parked twenty feet from your grave. There is no tombstone, only a flat marker with your name, the year of your birth, the year of your death and "Son of Rudolph and Viola." Nothing else. No touching lines about you being a beloved husband or caring father. I would say that the funeral director did a pretty accurate job with this inscription.

I stood there and looked at the fourteen-by-ten-inch granite marker and didn't know how to feel. I wasn't sad or angry, and only slightly afraid that you'd reach out and grab me as I knelt and cleaned some of the dirt away from the corners of what is clearly an unattended plot. Rationally, I knew you were not going to bust through your coffin to grab my wrists, but I still thought of all of the nightmares I've had, that my mother has had, that my brother and sisters have had . . . you've often threatened to come back from the dead to get us.

I'd like to say that this was a remarkable, life-changing moment. That finally visiting your grave after all these years had brought me closure. But that would be a lie. In fact, I felt very little. A little pity, perhaps—for a man buried in such an unremarkable manner, with no one but the groundskeeper visiting you and the other residents of this beautiful resting place.

It is beautiful, Dad.

Your grave is in a corner of a tree-lined cemetery. Farms surround the hillside. The grounds are impeccable. There are tombstones dating back to the 1800s, all in remarkable condition. I actually felt a bit of comfort in these surroundings.

I wonder, Dad, if you *had* outlived Rudy, would you have visited his grave? What would your thoughts have been? Would you have been relieved that he was dead? Would you have had any pity for your own monster? Would you have adorned his grave with flowers? I'm pretty sure you would have said a prayer, because as sinful as you were, you did seem to have some relationship with God. Maybe in your mind God was the only one who completely understood your pain and suffering, the only one who could atone for, or forgive, your actions. The rest of us certainly could not.

Of course, you never asked—that would have been a sign of weakness. You fought against showing any signs that you were not the toughest man in town.

That may have been your downfall.

As I drove away I reflected, searching for feeling. I didn't think it was normal—I had just visited your grave and, truly, felt no emotion. The only thing that kept running through my head was that Rudy—your father—one day told me, drunk of course, that you did not kill yourself, that you were murdered, just like our "uncle," Quebec Deputy Premier Pierre LaPorte. He said that when he found out who did it, he would hunt them down and kill them. I was around twelve when he told me this, and a bit on the naive side. Maybe I believed him? I'll give myself a bit of credit: I did not buy it wholeheartedly. But it did give me a bit of hope to think that my dad didn't take his own life—that he in fact died at the hands of the same FLQ fanatics who killed a Canadian politician during the October Crisis. What a fantasy. As a romantic and a storyteller, I would have loved it to be true.

Rudy told me this in the kitchen of the second-storey apartment he was living in at the time. To my recollection, it was the last time I saw him, because when I told my older and wiser brother of this he, for the first time, like a *real* father, forbade me from doing something. He told me I was not to see Rudy again. I honoured his request and did not even attend Rudy's funeral after he apparently took a tumble down the very steps that led to his apartment. Maybe he was murdered by the FLQ as well? More likely he was drunk and his story ended like so many other men of his ilk. Unspectacular and befitting, there will be no romanticizing of his death. He was a dangerous predator who should have died exactly the way I remember it. Alone at the bottom of a stairway that stank of urine. I may not be completely accurate in my facts, but let me have this one . . . He deserved nothing better in life, in death or in my memory.

I am not sure that you would disagree, Dad. You knew who he was. You lived with him until you could not live with him anymore. You fought him. You made him bleed. He made you bleed. He made your mother bleed. The rumour is that maybe he actually killed your mother. Did you know that? If you did not know, what would you have done if you had heard the stories? Apparently your mother was a saint. I have no recollection of her. I wish I did, because she is the common link between you and me. The rest of my family and yours, for the most part, are dark haired and dark eyed, like Rudy—or red haired and dark eyed like Grandma Molly. Not you and me. Blond. Blue-green eyes, probably much like Viola, my grandmother, who was of German descent. Strange, I didn't know her name until today, when I read it off of your grave marker.

What was she like, Dad? Was she kind? Was she a hard woman? Did you love her? How did you feel when she died? Did you suspect Rudy of any wrong-doing? I suppose she died in the early 1970s, because I was born in 1969 and don't recall meeting her. I believe I must have, but I think she died when I was very young. How do you think she would have reacted to your behaviour? Was she afraid of you? Did you cry at her funeral? Was it her death that veered you toward this life of alcohol, violence and philandering? You were born in 1946, so you were in your mid-twenties when she passed. I'm sure this had an impact on you, even if you weren't close. At least you got to grow to adulthood with her by your side. I never had that luxury. You didn't even give me the benefit of the decade mark before you decided to check out.

Before today I've never thought about your relationship with your mother. I have to believe that it must have been similar to the relationship I had with you, if only because you looked more like her than Rudy or your siblings. Is this what caused you some confusion? Did you feel different than the rest of your family? I understand that—I've always felt different than my siblings, and maybe they feel the same way. I looked different from them. I thought differently than them. I addressed problems in a different way than they did. I always felt that I was more LaPorte than Mulvihill (Mother's maiden name). I felt that even in my own family that I was an outcast. I was not one of their clan, I was one of yours. It was not a group I wanted to be associated with. I still don't. Maybe they felt that they didn't only not fit in with the rest of society as I did but also that they did not fit in with the one group that you were supposed to—family. I have struggled with this my entire life; it's nothing that they've done, it is all on me. My perception of how they view me. Of what they expect of me. Maybe it is all between my ears, but that's always been a very fertile place for ideas and conspiracies. It doesn't take much—I'm constantly creating scenarios, stories or concepts. It's great to be a bit of a dreamer, but it can also be so dangerous, Dad. I do believe that was part of your problem. Your fertile mind fabricated scenarios: Mom was cheating on you . . . some guy at the bar looked at you sideways . . . your boss was out to get you. Being creative is great, but it can also be a curse. A person can drive themselves crazy if they don't leave that space and bring themselves back down to reality. Maybe Rudy is the one who gave me complete access to the right side of my brain.

I'd like to think not, though—I'd rather not be grateful to a monster for providing me with the ability to create a story and put it on paper. In fact, I'm sure that's not the case . . . Grandpa Frankie was the one who could entertain an entire dance hall with his antics.

Did you have a good relationship with Frankie, Dad? How did you interact with him? How often did you sit at the kitchen table while he drank, smoked hand-rolled cigarettes and played the guitar? He was a storyteller. Jesus, he has been dead for thirty years and people still talk about him. *In a good way.* Why couldn't his positive energy bring you back from the dark places that you were visiting? I have a picture of you and Mom in Grandma and Grandpa's kitchen, but do not recall you interacting with either Frankie or Molly. I suspect they didn't like you. No one could hide what you were doing to their little girl or her children. Not sure what they could have done about it—Grandpa was five-foot-six at best, and I don't think he was much of a fighter. Grandma Molly, well, she would not hold back. I wonder how many times she gave you the business. I bet she did, and I bet you took it. She was a tough woman. A Scottish war bride with no room for your BS. She had seen tougher and probably let you know it.

Maybe this was the problem with your mother. Maybe she was tough and would not have tolerated your antics. Maybe you killed her. There's the fertile mind again, creating scenarios that likely have no relationship to reality . . . But you were a violent alcoholic, who shot at his own wife and kids . . . So, nothing is off the table.

Still, Dad, I am left wondering about your relation-ship with your mother. The mother-son bond is not easily broken. I do not recall you ever speaking of her. Why wouldn't you pass anything about her on to us? What could she have done to apparently make her disappear from your memory entirely?

Was she a good mother? Did she discipline you too harshly? Did she protect you from your own abusive father when you were a child? Or maybe she didn't do enough to protect you and your siblings from Rudy and you grew to resent her. Did you blame her for the fractured relationship that you had with your own dad? Maybe she suffered in silence while he did God knows what to you and your brothers and sisters. Am I reading too much into this? Am I filling a void in my own heart and mind with questions we both know will never be answered? I don't know . . . and maybe I don't want to.

THE LEDGE

If you've never been on one, you may not understand. Those of us who have, or who have thought about climbing out onto one, understand completely. We may not all call it "the ledge"—there are various ways of expressing it. I'm at rock bottom. The end of my rope. At my wits' end. Even simply, "I'm done."

To anyone who has completely and absolutely had enough, it's all the same thing. You're at the breaking point and have a very important choice to make. Do we accept the pain, noise and confusion that has taken residence in our minds and end it all? Do we ignore and quiet those noises and go on as though there is nothing troubling us? Or do we let someone talk us off the ledge and return to safety, trusting that it will all be better in the morning?

Those of us with someone to talk us off the ledge are fortunate. Those who stand alone are not. If there is no hand reaching out of the window trying to bring them back to safety, more often than not, there's a long, final step into oblivion. The fall lasts only seconds. The reverberations last a lifetime.

So, tell me, Dad, were you out on that ledge alone? Was the window simply closed or was there no one there to offer a hand? For all of the goddamned so-called friends you had, was there no one who recognized that you were maybe going through a difficult time? Did they ignore your cries for help or change in behaviour or attitude and just not show up?

Maybe you disguised it to the point where no one knew that you were struggling. We will never know.

While I've never allowed myself to be completely out on that ledge, I have been close. If we're honest, we all have, at one point or another. Mentally, we've all been out on that damn ledge. To physically put yourself out there, though— that's another level altogether. To work out the logistics of ending it all, of permanently quieting noises, is something entirely different.

I have never given any serious thought to it. I have very good friends who have. They have described moments where the despair is so great that in their minds the only answer is to not exist. The voices and noise may continue to echo, but they will not be around to hear.

So, what happens when we find ourselves climbing out onto that ledge, and there is no one to talk us down?

I found myself in a very difficult place mentally these past few weeks because of some new, stressful responsibilities at work. I've been hitting a few roadblocks in what I'm trying to do in a new role. Some of these problems I have created for myself. Some, others created. I'm not talking about total despair here, but I felt lost and defeated.

I found myself talking to myself on my commute home, before bed and even in my dreams, trying to resolve the problems I was facing. I finally had to ask, "What the hell is going on?" Am I going to let this situation control me, or am I going to control the situation? This type of pep talk is not always easy . . . It forced me to look at what I had done to contribute to the situation and to look at what I could have done differently. Sometimes the truthful answers are not exactly what our ego wants to hear; however, they are crucial to our own survival if we want to walk ourselves off of the ledge. The sad truth is, more often than not we are out on the ledge by ourselves. Not because no one wants to help us, but because the issues we are facing and the solutions to the problems are found between our own two ears. For the most part, we hold the key to the door behind which the answers lie.

I fully acknowledge that as I write this I struggle to follow my own advice. I am far from perfect. I struggle daily to stay on course. It is not easy, and if I were a psychologist I would not be my best patient.

I want to be happy. I want others to be happy. I tell my kids that they choose to have a good or bad day. They can choose to be happy or sad. Pie in the sky, maybe, but two days ago Suzie had to repeatedly ask if I was okay. Was something bothering me? Finally, in bed after a long day, she cuddled up to me and said: "I don't like it when you are sad." We lay there for a long time. Me holding her, her holding me; and I tried to reassure her that I was okay, that

I wasn't sad. But she knew. I was not myself. I was having one of my *off* days. We all have them, and it's okay—we are entitled to them. We've earned them. But as I've said, for people like us, our partners, spouses and children pay the price for those days. They did not sign up for this. It has nothing to do with them, but they have to deal with it. It's not fair.

Dad, did you feel this when you came home after a long day working at the garage, the mine or whatever job you happened to hold? Is this the reason why on many days you simply did not come home and instead elected to go to the bar to drink with your buddies? Was it easier to shoot pool or get into a fight and get your frustrations out that way than to come home to five hungry kids and a wife who simply wanted to talk to another adult after being cooped up all day with all those children? I suppose that is why a lot of men and women choose to stop by the local pub on their way home from work rather face the reality of a home life that is less than perfect. I won't pretend to understand, but I can see how this option may be more attractive than the thought of going home and facing problems head-on.

I've talked myself off of the ledge more times than I care to admit. Again, I was not ever in danger of really hurting myself physically, but emotionally I was not doing myself any favours. I've had many sleepless nights because of the pressures I was experiencing at one point or another. Thankfully for me, most are business related. For other people, the pressures are personal. It may seem odd to think that my issues did not start and end with the horrors that I experienced during my childhood. I have to agree, but up until I began writing this book, I had parked all of these memories deep in a vault. I felt and still feel, to a point, that I had addressed these issues and properly stashed the memories. To me, there was no reason to relive the past. I couldn't change it, so energy spent reflecting on it was wasted. I moved on as coldly as a serial killer moves on to his next victim.

THE DARKNESS

I expect, Dad, that if you were alive and you and I were able to have an honest conversation about darkness, that you would have much to say. I wish you were here to compare notes with. This is not to say that I am eternally dark, but I cannot lie and say that there aren't times when the darkness does not envelop me. The strange thing with the darkness is that while it is cold and harsh, it's also somehow comforting. Seductive. I can't really explain it and would love to be able to understand the power of melancholy, why it's both painful and satisfying. For some reason, the suffering brings ease to my mind, body and soul. As I've said, I believe I am forever cutting myself, just not with a razor. I purposefully listen to dark songs that take me to places I don't want to visit. I drive by the places where I've been abused, shot at and neglected. The funny thing is I do not resist. I grab that shadowy figure by the hand and let it lead me down its treacherous path with no thought of repercussions.

Did you have the same experience, Dad? Were you triggered by a song, smell or image that, like a magnet, drew you and your emotions to a place that you were trying hard to avoid, but knew you belonged? Was it so hard for you to accept that it was okay to be happy that you not only ran from the light but dove headlong into the darkness?

What is it about this dark place that is so welcoming to so many? I've seen photos of you, Dad, and honestly, you look like hell. Like you were either living in hell or had just came back. Your eyes have not even the slightest glimmer of life. I'm not sure how it's possible, but your blue-green eyes seem dark. They're shadowy, always: there is no life in them. No optimism. No future. When did you fall into the pit of despair? Were you already serving a prison sentence and had no reasonable expectation of release? Was it life without parole? More accurately, was it life without life? Did you see the writing on the wall?

How bad could things have been for you that you had already seen your future and knew how it would end? Was that blanket of darkness so inviting, so tempting, that you had resigned yourself to your terrible and tragic end? Could you see no other way out? Was there no light, Dad?

I've seen the darkness too. I've been in the darkness, Dad, and while it's inviting, I resist it when I can. Some days it's easy to resist. Some days I embrace it like it's a long-lost relative. A father maybe? Of course, whenever I do enter the void the only people who suffer are my wife and children. Now, they don't necessarily know what is going on, but they have come to understand that while physically I'm in the same room as them, emotionally I am on some desolate, barren planet where I don't want or, more importantly, don't have to talk. I can just exist in a world where, if I choose, I only have to worry about . . . me. No outside influences. No questions to be answered. No work to be done. I can sit in that darkness and just be. Strange how a person trying to find peace of mind can go from a man sitting in paradise, enjoying all of God's gifts, to a dark, cold place . . . and stranger that the result is the exact same: a person, alone with their thoughts, and no one to harm them, no one to love them, no one to affect them, no one to judge them. It's a terribly wonderful place to visit, but an equally awful place to live. And while I do spend some time there, I've never moved in. Is this what happened to you, Dad? Did you find the place so damn peaceful that you took up residence in the desolation? Is that why you were so detached from all of us? Had you already put your stuff on shelves and moved in lock, stock and barrel? What could have happened to you that you simply said, "I'm done"? Did you choose to put the black cloak around your shoulders for your remaining years rather than try to find even the smallest of reasons to live?

I know others have experienced this darkness the way I have. And it's not as inviting as it seems. It's not euphoric. It is the opposite. The evil that lurks there is inviting and comforting and seems to offer all of the answers. It does not. It offers only questions . . . questions that cannot be answered. The questions are the most dangerous part of the darkness.

I shared this passage with a very dear friend who suffers from depression. He was concerned that I might be trivializing the illness, that I was suggesting my darkness was akin to clinical depression. I assured him I was not. The darkness, for me, is not depression. I do not know what depression feels like. (He has told me, repeatedly over our twenty-year relationship: "I'm glad you don't.")

I indulge melancholy. While some of the experiences and feelings may be similar, what I am describing is not depression. My darkness is a willed mental state. Depression is a lethal combination of anguish and a chemical imbalance. I've seen the results of the disease first-hand, Dad, and I do believe that *you* suffered from depression.

DEPRESSION

Depression is a topic that is discussed now more than it ever has been. It is accepted that people suffer from and live with mental illness and, for the most part, are not shunned by society as they may have been back in your day.

I think we can both agree that you suffered from one form of mental illness, Dad, most likely depression. As I sit here and see the folks coming forward acknowledging that they suffer from depression, I wonder what your adult life may have been like if you'd been able to address the issue out in the open.

I'm not sure that you would ever have admitted that you suffered from mental illness. That sometimes you felt sad. So sad that you could see no end to the pain you were feeling. The despair must have been unbearable. Clearly, it was.

I have two very good friends who suffer from clinical depression, and they tell me they would never wish this on their worst enemy. I tell them I don't understand it; when I'm feeling blue, I force myself to focus on the positive things in my life—my wife, my kids, my job, my friends. To this, they both say the same thing: they're glad I don't understand what they have been through and what they are sure to go through again.

They don't always know when a bout of depression is going to hit them, and they do not know how they are going to respond to it.

Both are now medicated. Both react differently to the medication and, frankly, both, based on what I see from my time with them, suffer very differently during their bouts of depression. I do not believe there is one "treatment" for depression but do believe the result of so many attempts to treat it—or leaving it untreated—is too often and too tragically the same.

They want the pain to end. They don't care how it ends; the pain they're feeling is overwhelming, and they just want it to be done with.

Is this what you were feeling, Dad, when you decided to put that gun in your mouth?

Were the voices in your head just too much for you to bear?

What movie was replaying in your mind when you made the ultimate decision?

Were you thinking of all the mistakes you had made throughout your life?

Were you thinking of your wife and five children living in a tent trailer by the side of a road when you loaded the fatal shell?

Did memories of you beating my mother enter into your mind as you pulled that trigger?

You know, Dad, I'm not going to simply chalk up your final action to depression, even though I know I could. No, it's not that simple.

There are millions of adults who live with depression every day and take the steps to deal with it. Especially within our own family. Sure, I don't suffer the way my friends do, or the way that many other people do, but that doesn't exclude me from this group.

I've said it before, and I'll say it again: I do not fear death. Nor do I welcome it. I just know that when my number is called, I'll accept it. But I'm not jumping the line to get ahead of anyone.

I had an experience in Florida years ago with a couple of friends. One who is as tough as you ever were, and both he and I were loaded. Another friend was driving us home—him to his trailer and me to my hotel. This strong, tough man started crying about his life and threatening suicide. I was beside myself. Maybe it was my PTSD kicking in, I honestly do not know. I called him out and told him my personal belief, that committing suicide was selfish. That suicide may resolve his issues, but the people he left behind would have to deal with the repercussions of his actions for the rest of their lives.

I accept the criticism I'll likely face for having said these things, but I speak frankly and honestly as the son of someone who killed himself to the devastation wreaked by the act.

I was so passionate and firm in my belief, that I threatened to take my friend out of the truck and beat the shit out of him if he kept talking about killing himself. There is no doubt that he would have kicked my ass six ways to Sunday, but I was willing to risk that in order to prove to him that suicide was not the answer.

In my view, it was the easy way out.

Maybe I'm wrong.

I don't really know as I've never been so despondent that I wanted to just end it all.

I can tell you that I've arrested suicidal people, spoken to friends who are very close to committing suicide and I do tell them the same thing. The collateral damage is way more than they can imagine.

It's okay to be sad. It's okay to feel despondent. It is okay to feel that the whole world is crashing down on you.

It is not okay to quit.

I encourage them to do what I have done, which is to recognize the crisis and acknowledge that it is not good. I ask them (and myself when I've been at rock bottom) what is the worst-case scenario? . . . Do you lose your wife, your job, your house? Okay . . . it is a mess, but there are ways and opportunities to replace just about anything in your life . . . anything other than . . . your life.

Pulling that trigger or tying the knot or taking the pills do not solve the problem. As I see it, they just transfer the problem to those who survive. It is critical of me to say to those considering or who have considered ending their own life: what you are thinking of doing does not change a damn thing.

Trust me, the people you love most are the ones who have to pick up the pieces. Parents of teens who have committed suicide have to live their entire lives questioning their actions; spouses have to wonder what they could have done differently . . . children are left to write letters to their deceased parents forty years after the fact.

It's not pretty.

If I could talk to my despondent friend today I'd still likely want to tell him to "tough it out," but I know that is not the correct message. Instead, I'd say: you are not alone. There are people out there, even though you may not realize it in the moment, that care about you. That love you. That want to spend time with you. They want just one more cup of coffee with you. One more drive in a car, one more hockey game. They just want to see you smile. They want to look into your eyes and see hope, joy, sadness and, yes, even despair. They, we, want to share in your moments of happiness and more importantly your moments of pain. We love you.

We want to hold you. Want to assure you that while everything appears to be bleak there is something better in the days to come. We want to let you know that if you control the sadness and despair that you can try to decide to either be sad or happy. Now we also know that there are medical reasons for your illness and that you are not choosing to be sad . . . But you can choose to accept our help and walk with us to a professional who can try to treat you and hopefully get you to a place where clarity rules and allow the darkest storms to pass with us by your side.

Dad, I wish I was able to express this to you before you decided to put that bullet in your head. I know you did some very bad things, but I honestly don't believe you were a bad man.

Do you remember that day when I curled up in your lap in the doorway of that farmhouse we lived in out in Horton?

You had returned from a bender; you were gone for God knows how many days and doing God knows what. You came into the kitchen. Mom was there. I don't remember any conversation at all. No fighting. No arguing. I don't remember who else was there, but you sat down in the doorway between the kitchen and the living room. There was no door, just a wide door frame. You sat on the floor, with your back against one side of the frame and your feet propped on the other. I looked at you and noticed that your eyes were red and wet. You were crying.

This was about two, maybe three years before you killed yourself.

You just sat there, looking despondent and alone. My seven-year-old heart went out to you, and I crawled up on your lap and asked you if you were okay. I could see the pain in your blue-green eyes and just wanted to let you know that I loved you. You did not speak. You just held me close. I'll never forget that, Dad.

One of my regrets is that I was not able to crawl up on your lap in that trailer where you ended it all and tell you that everything was going to be okay. I wish I could have been there to wipe away your tears and to take that goddamned gun out of your hands. I wish the nine-year-old me had the knowledge that the fifty-one-year-old me has so that I could have pulled you aside and got you the help that you clearly needed. Jesus Christ, Dad, I wish I could have done more.

I'm sorry.

Acknowledgements

I would like to thank Suzie, Angèle and Eric for their love, patience and understanding as I wrote this very emotional book.

Barrie, Monique, Doris and Sally—my siblings—thank you for always being there and for allowing me to share our story with the world. I know this is not easy, but know that by sharing with others who are, at this very moment, experiencing what we experienced forty years ago, we share hope.

Michael, I appreciate our friendship first and foremost, but also your guidance, and reassurance that this work may offer some comfort.

I also wish to thank friends and family, past and present, who accept me for who I am. My hope is that you understand where I've come from and where I am going.

A special thank you goes to the friends who have provided me with advice on how to address depression with honesty and compassion. Your input was invaluable.

Lastly, to all the survivors who have stood and said "Me Too"—your actions, words and strength gave me the courage to write when I felt most vulnerable: thank you.